SPENDING PLANNER

BY SHONVERSATION

I HOPE THE WAY YOU SPEND YOUR MONEY IS IN LINE WITH THE TRUTH OF WHO YOU ARE AND WHAT YOU CARE ABOUT. I HOPE THAT YOUR MONEY BRINGS JOY TO YOU AND THE ONES YOU LOVE. AND I HOPE YOU USE IT AS A POWERFUL FORCE FOR GOOD TO FULFILL YOUR BEST INTENTIONS.

- Oprah Winfrey

Inside the Shonversation Spending Planner

It's true, budgeting makes it possible to achieve your short-term and long-term financial goals but following a budget can also help you accurately determine which bills to expect on a regular basis so that you can plan accordingly. Some people find that planning ahead helps reduce bill-related anxiety. The Shonversation Spending Planner enables you to track the amount of income you generate as well as record outgoing bills and expenses.

Below, we briefly discuss the sections you'll find in the Shonversation Spending Planner. The planner is easy to use. All of the sections are straight-forward and simple to complete on a weekly, bi-weekly, or monthly basis.

NET WORTH STATEMENT

The net worth statement allows you to take an honest look at your entire financial situation — what you own and what you owe. If your assets are larger than your liabilities, you have a "positive" net worth. If your liabilities are larger than your assets, you have a "negative" net worth.

PERIODIC EXPENSES

Use the 12 month calendar to record upcoming periodic expenses, such as those related to moving/relocating, down payments, insurance policy renewals, etc.

ANNUAL BILL TRACKER

Use the Annual Bill Tracker to record expenses paid each month. Record the day of the month the bill is due and the amount. Check off the month once the bill is paid.

52-WEEK HOUSEHOLD INCOME WORKSHEET

It's important to get a clear picture of how much you have coming in every month in order to better budget your bills and possibly save toward your goals. Use the 52-Week Household Income worksheet to record the total amount of income you receive each week for an entire year.

DEBT ORGANIZER WORKSHEET

The first step in managing and reducing your debt is to make a list of who you owe money to and how much you owe them. Use the Debt Organizer worksheet to list the debts you owe.

DEBT PAYOFF GOAL WORKSHEET

Use the Debt Payoff Goal worksheet to record the total amount paid toward debt each month above the minimum payment due.

52-WEEK SAVINGS TRACKER

Use the 52-week Savings Tracker to record the total amount saved each week for an entire year.

52-WEEK SAVINGS CHALLENGES

Use either of the savings worksheets to challenge yourself to save.

BILL AND INCOME CALENDAR

- Gather all the bills you pay in one month to determine your regular monthly expenses. Remember to include any bills that are paid automatically.

- In advance of the due date, write the date when you must send the payment or when the money must be taken out of your account. If you're paying by mail, mark the due date at least seven days before it is due. For in-person or online bill payment, mark two or three days before the due date to ensure you are not late.

- Write down the name of the company or person you owe the money to and the amount that's due on the date the bill must be sent to arrive on time.

- Once you have finished adding your bills, add your sources of income as well. Write in the dates and amounts you get paid or when you receive other income. Use the Bill Calendar to compare your weekly bill total to your weekly income total. If you have more bills than income in a given week, consider asking to change the due dates of some of your bills.

WEEKLY SPENDING PLAN WORKSHEET

Use the Weekly Spending Plan worksheet to record:

- Income - record the source of income and the amount.
- Bills & Expenses - record who you're paying, the amount, and the method of payment.
- Cash Envelopes - record the expense category and the amount.
- Savings/Sinking Funds - record the amount saved and the purpose of the savings.
- Debt Repayment - record the total amount paid toward debt that week above the minimum payment due.
- Weekly Summary - at the end of each week, calculate the total amount of income received and subtract the total amount of bills, cash expenses, savings, and debt payments to determine the remaining amount that will roll over to the following week.
- Weekly Spending Log - track the individual amounts spent on purchases such as food, clothing, self-care, etc.

MONTHLY SPENDING SUMMARY

Use the Monthly Spending Summary to calculate all monthly expenses. The Monthly Spending Summary will provide a quick overview of income vs expenses---giving you the opportunity to determine whether adjustments need to be made to your spending plan.

30-DAY NO SPEND CHALLENGE

Use the 30-Day No Spend tracker to record each day that you do not make an impulse or non-essential purchase.

ANNUAL TRACKERS

Net Worth *statement*

Take an honest look at your entire financial situation — what you own and what you owe. This is a "net worth statement." On one side, list what you own. These are your "assets. " On the other side, list what you owe. These are your "liabilities" or debts. Subtract your liabilities from your assets. If your assets are larger than your liabilities, you have a "positive" net worth. If your liabilities are larger than your assets, you have a "negative" net worth.

Evaluate

The first step in developing a money management plan is to evaluate your current situation. An excellent way to do this is to prepare a net worth statement. The Net Worth worksheet on the following page can be used to add together your assets (what you own) and subtract from that the sum of your liabilities (what you owe). Space is provided for you to calculate your net worth statement now and again 1 year from now.

Assets

To determine the value of your assets, start with cash available. Include your checking and saving accounts. Now list all your investments, including bonds, mutual funds, life insurance cash values, and others. List additional assets, using the current market value for your house, real estate, automobiles, jewelry, antiques, and other personal items.

Liabilities

To determine your liabilities, list the amount that you owe to all your creditors and lenders. Remember to include current bills, charge accounts, mortgage balance, and loans against your life insurance.

Net Worth

By subtracting liabilities from assets, you can determine your net worth. Look closely at your final net worth figure. Do you own more than you owe? Consider what you would like this figure to be a year from now. What do you need to do to achieve that goal?

Prepare a new net worth statement at the same time each year to reflect the changes in your finances. The market value of your assets may have declined or risen. You may have paid off one loan or gained another.

Net Worth *statement*

Year One

ASSETS	VALUE
Cash	
Money in savings	
Money in checking	
Money in CDs	
Money market accounts	
Annuities	
Cash value of life insurance	
Stocks	
Bonds	
Mutual funds	
Employee pensions	
IRAs	
401(k) and similar plans	
Primary home	
Vacation home	
Investment properties	
Resale value of car #1	
Resale value of car #2	
Boats/recreational vehicles	
Jewelry	
Art, antiques, collectibles	
Furniture	
ASSET TOTAL	

LIABILITIES	BALANCE
Primary mortgage	
Vacation home mortgage	
Home equity loan(s)	
Investment home mortgage	
Car loan #1	
Car loan #2	
Credit card #1	
Credit card #2	
Credit card #3	
Student loan(s)	
Bank loan(s)	
Private loan(s)	
Medical bills	
Taxes owed	
LIABILITIES TOTAL	

$	Total assets
$	- Total liabilities
$	**=NET WORTH**

COMPLETION DATE:

Net Worth *statement*

Year Two

ASSETS	VALUE
Cash	
Money in savings	
Money in checking	
Money in CDs	
Money market accounts	
Annuities	
Cash value of life insurance	
Stocks	
Bonds	
Mutual funds	
Employee pensions	
IRAs	
401(k) and similar plans	
Primary home	
Vacation home	
Investment properties	
Resale value of car #1	
Resale value of car #2	
Boats/recreational vehicles	
Jewelry	
Art, antiques, collectibles	
Furniture	
ASSET TOTAL	

LIABILITIES	BALANCE
Primary mortgage	
Vacation home mortgage	
Home equity loan(s)	
Investment home mortgage	
Car loan #1	
Car loan #2	
Credit card #1	
Credit card #2	
Credit card #3	
Student loan(s)	
Bank loan(s)	
Private loan(s)	
Medical bills	
Taxes owed	
LIABILITIES TOTAL	

$	Total assets
$	- Total liabilities
$	**=NET WORTH**

COMPLETION DATE:

Periodic *expenses*

Record any expenditures that are paid on a quarterly, semi-annual, or annual basis. Examples include life insurance, car registration, vacations, etc.

YEAR:

January	February	March	April
May	**June**	**July**	**August**
September	**October**	**November**	**December**

Annual Bill *tracker*

PAY TO	DUE DATE	AMOUNT	Jan	Feb	Mar	Apr	May	Jun	Jul	Aug	Sep	Oct	Nov	Dec
			☐	☐	☐	☐	☐	☐	☐	☐	☐	☐	☐	☐
			☐	☐	☐	☐	☐	☐	☐	☐	☐	☐	☐	☐
			☐	☐	☐	☐	☐	☐	☐	☐	☐	☐	☐	☐
			☐	☐	☐	☐	☐	☐	☐	☐	☐	☐	☐	☐
			☐	☐	☐	☐	☐	☐	☐	☐	☐	☐	☐	☐
			☐	☐	☐	☐	☐	☐	☐	☐	☐	☐	☐	☐
			☐	☐	☐	☐	☐	☐	☐	☐	☐	☐	☐	☐
			☐	☐	☐	☐	☐	☐	☐	☐	☐	☐	☐	☐
			☐	☐	☐	☐	☐	☐	☐	☐	☐	☐	☐	☐
			☐	☐	☐	☐	☐	☐	☐	☐	☐	☐	☐	☐
			☐	☐	☐	☐	☐	☐	☐	☐	☐	☐	☐	☐
			☐	☐	☐	☐	☐	☐	☐	☐	☐	☐	☐	☐
			☐	☐	☐	☐	☐	☐	☐	☐	☐	☐	☐	☐
			☐	☐	☐	☐	☐	☐	☐	☐	☐	☐	☐	☐
			☐	☐	☐	☐	☐	☐	☐	☐	☐	☐	☐	☐
			☐	☐	☐	☐	☐	☐	☐	☐	☐	☐	☐	☐
			☐	☐	☐	☐	☐	☐	☐	☐	☐	☐	☐	☐
			☐	☐	☐	☐	☐	☐	☐	☐	☐	☐	☐	☐
			☐	☐	☐	☐	☐	☐	☐	☐	☐	☐	☐	☐
			☐	☐	☐	☐	☐	☐	☐	☐	☐	☐	☐	☐
			☐	☐	☐	☐	☐	☐	☐	☐	☐	☐	☐	☐
			☐	☐	☐	☐	☐	☐	☐	☐	☐	☐	☐	☐
			☐	☐	☐	☐	☐	☐	☐	☐	☐	☐	☐	☐
			☐	☐	☐	☐	☐	☐	☐	☐	☐	☐	☐	☐
			☐	☐	☐	☐	☐	☐	☐	☐	☐	☐	☐	☐
			☐	☐	☐	☐	☐	☐	☐	☐	☐	☐	☐	☐
			☐	☐	☐	☐	☐	☐	☐	☐	☐	☐	☐	☐
			☐	☐	☐	☐	☐	☐	☐	☐	☐	☐	☐	☐
			☐	☐	☐	☐	☐	☐	☐	☐	☐	☐	☐	☐

Annual Bill *tracker*

PAY TO	DUE DATE	AMOUNT	Jan	Feb	Mar	Apr	May	Jun	Jul	Aug	Sep	Oct	Nov	Dec
			☐	☐	☐	☐	☐	☐	☐	☐	☐	☐	☐	☐
			☐	☐	☐	☐	☐	☐	☐	☐	☐	☐	☐	☐
			☐	☐	☐	☐	☐	☐	☐	☐	☐	☐	☐	☐
			☐	☐	☐	☐	☐	☐	☐	☐	☐	☐	☐	☐
			☐	☐	☐	☐	☐	☐	☐	☐	☐	☐	☐	☐
			☐	☐	☐	☐	☐	☐	☐	☐	☐	☐	☐	☐
			☐	☐	☐	☐	☐	☐	☐	☐	☐	☐	☐	☐
			☐	☐	☐	☐	☐	☐	☐	☐	☐	☐	☐	☐
			☐	☐	☐	☐	☐	☐	☐	☐	☐	☐	☐	☐
			☐	☐	☐	☐	☐	☐	☐	☐	☐	☐	☐	☐
			☐	☐	☐	☐	☐	☐	☐	☐	☐	☐	☐	☐
			☐	☐	☐	☐	☐	☐	☐	☐	☐	☐	☐	☐
			☐	☐	☐	☐	☐	☐	☐	☐	☐	☐	☐	☐
			☐	☐	☐	☐	☐	☐	☐	☐	☐	☐	☐	☐
			☐	☐	☐	☐	☐	☐	☐	☐	☐	☐	☐	☐
			☐	☐	☐	☐	☐	☐	☐	☐	☐	☐	☐	☐
			☐	☐	☐	☐	☐	☐	☐	☐	☐	☐	☐	☐
			☐	☐	☐	☐	☐	☐	☐	☐	☐	☐	☐	☐
			☐	☐	☐	☐	☐	☐	☐	☐	☐	☐	☐	☐
			☐	☐	☐	☐	☐	☐	☐	☐	☐	☐	☐	☐
			☐	☐	☐	☐	☐	☐	☐	☐	☐	☐	☐	☐
			☐	☐	☐	☐	☐	☐	☐	☐	☐	☐	☐	☐
			☐	☐	☐	☐	☐	☐	☐	☐	☐	☐	☐	☐
			☐	☐	☐	☐	☐	☐	☐	☐	☐	☐	☐	☐
			☐	☐	☐	☐	☐	☐	☐	☐	☐	☐	☐	☐
			☐	☐	☐	☐	☐	☐	☐	☐	☐	☐	☐	☐
			☐	☐	☐	☐	☐	☐	☐	☐	☐	☐	☐	☐
			☐	☐	☐	☐	☐	☐	☐	☐	☐	☐	☐	☐
			☐	☐	☐	☐	☐	☐	☐	☐	☐	☐	☐	☐

Monthly *income*

Your income and benefits provide you with the financial resources to pay for your living expenses. It's important to get a clear picture of how much you have coming in every month in order to budget your bills and possibly save toward your goals.

Income may not always come on a regular basis. Knowing what income is regular, irregular, seasonal, and one-time-only can help you be prepared for when you have less coming in.

Regular Income

Total all money you will receive. Begin with regular income that you and your family receive—wages, salaries, income earned from a business, Security benefits, pension payments, alimony, child support, veterans' benefits, public assistance payments, unemployment compensation, allowances, and any other income.

Variable Income

Include variable income, such as interest from bank accounts and investments, dividends from stock and insurance, rents from property you own, gifts, and money from any other sources.

Irregular Income

If your earnings are irregular, it may be more difficult to estimate your income. It is better to underestimate than overestimate income when setting up a budget. Some households have sufficient income, but its receipt does not coincide with the arrival of bills. For these households, planning is very important.

What to do

- Gather all of your pay stubs, benefit statements, and records of electronic payments.

- Enter the amount of income or benefits you receive in the appropriate week of the month.

52-Week Household *income*

Estimated Annual Income $

Year

Actual Annual Income $

Week	Income Received
1	
2	
3	
4	
5	
6	
7	
8	
9	
10	
11	
12	
13	
14	
15	
16	
17	
18	
19	
20	
21	
22	
23	
24	
25	
26	

Week	Income Received
27	
28	
29	
30	
31	
32	
33	
34	
35	
36	
37	
38	
39	
40	
41	
42	
43	
44	
45	
46	
47	
48	
49	
50	
51	
52	

Your income and benefits provide you with the financial resources to pay for your living expenses. It's important to get a clear picture of how much you have coming in every month in order to budget your bills and possibly save toward your goals.

Fill in the net income amount you receive each week and write that in as the weekly total.

Types of Income to Consider

Salary/hourly wages
Bonuses or commissions
Investment income
Side hustle income
Credit card rewards
Alimony
Child support
Boarder income
Capital gains income
Disability income
Foster-care income
Housing or parsonage allowance
Interest and dividends income
Notes receivable income
Retirement, annuity, pension income
Royalty payments
Social security income
Temporary leave income
Tip income
Trust income
Public assistance income
Unemployment benefits
VA benefits

Debt *organizer*

The first step in managing and reducing your debt is to make a list of who you owe money to and how much you owe them. Be sure to include debts owed to friends and family, credit card companies, banks, etc.

What to do

- Gather all of your bills and loan statements to help you figure out what you owe.
- Get a copy of your credit report. This can help you find any debt you may have forgotten about or has been sent to collections.

Priority	DEBT/CREDITOR	Total Amount Borrowed	ACCOUNT BALANCE	Monthly Payment	Payoff Goal Date
			$		
			$		
			$		
			$		
			$		
			$		
			$		
			$		
			$		
			$		
			$		
			$		
			$		
			$		
			$		
			$		
			$		
			$		
			$		
			$		
			$		
			$		
			$		
			$		

Debt *organizer*

Priority	DEBT/CREDITOR	Total Amount Borrowed	**ACCOUNT BALANCE**	Monthly Payment	Payoff Goal Date
			$		
			$		
			$		
			$		
			$		
			$		
			$		
			$		
			$		
			$		
			$		
			$		
			$		
			$		
			$		
			$		
			$		
			$		
			$		
			$		
			$		
			$		
			$		
			$		
			$		
			$		
			$		
			$		
			$		
			$		
			$		

Debt Payoff *goals*

Total amount of debt owed:	Debt payoff goal(s):
Dollar amount you'd like to pay off this year:	

Fill in the amount paid on your debt (above the minimum due) for each month listed below.

JAN — Total amount paid toward debt:

FEB — Total amount paid toward debt:

MAR — Total amount paid toward debt:

APR — Total amount paid toward debt:

MAY — Total amount paid toward debt:

JUN — Total amount paid toward debt:

JUL — Total amount paid toward debt:

AUG — Total amount paid toward debt:

SEP — Total amount paid toward debt:

OCT — Total amount paid toward debt:

NOV — Total amount paid toward debt:

DEC — Total amount paid toward debt:

52-Week Savings *tracker*

52-week savings goal: $

Weekly amount to save: $

Week	Deposit Amount	Savings Balance	Goal Met
1			○
2			○
3			○
4			○
5			○
6			○
7			○
8			○
9			○
10			○
11			○
12			○
13			○
14			○
15			○
16			○
17			○
18			○
19			○
20			○
21			○
22			○
23			○
24			○
25			○
26			○

Week	Deposit Amount	Savings Balance	Goal Met
27			○
28			○
29			○
30			○
31			○
32			○
33			○
34			○
35			○
36			○
37			○
38			○
39			○
40			○
41			○
42			○
43			○
44			○
45			○
46			○
47			○
48			○
49			○
50			○
51			○
52			○

52-Week Nickel *challenge*

SAVINGS TARGET: $3,339.75

START DATE:

END DATE:

I have decided to do the 52-week nickel savings challenge because...

....

....

....

....

....

Which daily/weekly purchases can I eliminate in order to cover the nickel challenge deposits?

1. ....
2. ....
3. ....
4. ....
5. ....
6. ....
7. ....

WEEK	SAVED	BALANCE	WEEK	SAVED	BALANCE
1	$1.40	$1.40	27	$65.10	$897.75
2	$3.85	$5.25	28	$67.55	$965.30
3	$6.30	$11.55	29	$70.00	$1035.30
4	$8.75	$20.30	30	$72.45	$1107.75
5	$11.20	$31.50	31	$74.90	$1182.65
6	$13.65	$45.15	32	$77.35	$1260.00
7	$16.10	$61.25	33	$79.80	$1339.80
8	$18.55	$79.80	34	$82.25	$1422.05
9	$21.00	$100.80	35	$84.70	$1506.75
10	$23.45	$124.25	36	$87.15	$1593.90
11	$25.90	$150.15	37	$89.60	$1683.50
12	$28.35	$178.50	38	$92.05	$1775.55
13	$30.80	$209.30	39	$94.50	$1870.05
14	$33.25	$242.55	40	$96.95	$1967.00
15	$35.70	$278.25	41	$99.40	$2066.40
16	$38.15	$316.40	42	$101.85	$2168.25
17	$40.60	$357.00	43	$104.30	$2272.55
18	$43.05	$400.05	44	$106.75	$2379.30
19	$45.50	$445.55	45	$109.20	$2488.50
20	$47.95	$493.50	46	$111.65	$2600.15
21	$50.40	$543.90	47	$114.10	$2714.25
22	$52.85	$596.75	48	$116.55	$2830.80
23	$55.30	$652.05	49	$119.00	$2949.80
24	$57.75	$709.80	50	$121.45	$3071.25
25	$60.20	$770.00	51	$123.90	$3195.15
26	$62.65	$832.65	52	$144.60	$3339.75

notes

52-Week Savings *challenge*

Week	Deposit	Balance	Week	Deposit	Balance	Week	Deposit	Balance
☐ 1	$1	$1	☐ 18	$18	$171	☐ 35	$35	$630
☐ 2	$2	$3	☐ 19	$19	$190	☐ 36	$36	$666
☐ 3	$3	$6	☐ 20	$20	$210	☐ 37	$37	$703
☐ 4	$4	$10	☐ 21	$21	$231	☐ 38	$38	$741
☐ 5	$5	$15	☐ 22	$22	$253	☐ 39	$39	$780
☐ 6	$6	$21	☐ 23	$23	$276	☐ 40	$40	$820
☐ 7	$7	$28	☐ 24	$24	$300	☐ 41	$41	$861
☐ 8	$8	$36	☐ 25	$25	$325	☐ 42	$42	$903
☐ 9	$9	$45	☐ 26	$26	$351	☐ 43	$43	$946
☐ 10	$10	$55	☐ 27	$27	$378	☐ 44	$44	$990
☐ 11	$11	$66	☐ 28	$28	$406	☐ 45	$45	$1,035
☐ 12	$12	$78	☐ 29	$29	$435	☐ 46	$46	$1,081
☐ 13	$13	$91	☐ 30	$30	$465	☐ 47	$47	$1,128
☐ 14	$14	$105	☐ 31	$31	$496	☐ 48	$48	$1,176
☐ 15	$15	$120	☐ 32	$32	$528	☐ 49	$49	$1,225
☐ 16	$16	$136	☐ 33	$33	$561	☐ 50	$50	$1,275
☐ 17	$17	$153	☐ 34	$34	$595	☐ 51	$51	$1,326
					Success!	☐ 52	$52	$1,378

notes

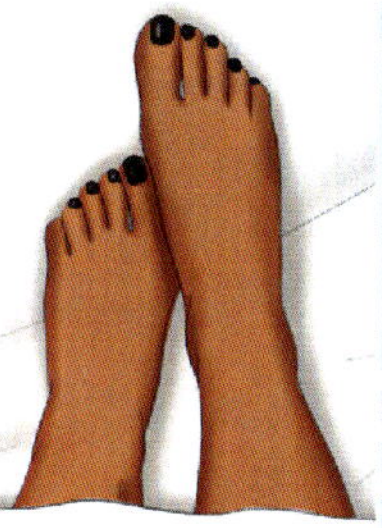

Account *passwords*

WEBSITE	USERNAME	PASSWORD	LINKED EMAIL

MONTH ONE

Bill and Income *calendar*

FINANCIAL GOALS

MONDAY	TUESDAY	WEDNESDAY

JAN FEB MAR APR MAY JUN JUL AUG SEP OCT NOV DEC

THURSDAY	FRIDAY	SATURDAY	SUNDAY

Spending *Plan*

Week of:

INCOME		Salary/Wages	Investment	Business	Side-Hustle
INCOME SOURCE	AMOUNT				
Rollover from previous week		☐	☐	☐	☐
		☐	☐	☐	☐
		☐	☐	☐	☐
		☐	☐	☐	☐
		☐	☐	☐	☐
		☐	☐	☐	☐
		☐	☐	☐	☐
(A) TOTAL	$				

BILLS & EXPENSES		Cash	Credit Card	Debit	Check
PAY TO	AMOUNT				
		☐	☐	☐	☐
		☐	☐	☐	☐
		☐	☐	☐	☐
		☐	☐	☐	☐
		☐	☐	☐	☐
		☐	☐	☐	☐
		☐	☐	☐	☐
		☐	☐	☐	☐
		☐	☐	☐	☐
		☐	☐	☐	☐
		☐	☐	☐	☐
		☐	☐	☐	☐
		☐	☐	☐	☐
		☐	☐	☐	☐
		☐	☐	☐	☐
(B) TOTAL	$				

Financial Priorities

This week's financial goal(s)

CASH ENVELOPES							
CATEGORY	AMOUNT	BANKING WITHDRAWAL DENOMINATIONS					
		$1	$5	$10	$20	$50	$100
		DENOMINATION TOTAL					
(C) TOTAL	$						

SAVINGS/SINKING FUNDS

ACCOUNT	AMOUNT	Sinking Fund	Short Term	Long Term	Retirement
		☐	☐	☐	☐
		☐	☐	☐	☐
		☐	☐	☐	☐
		☐	☐	☐	☐
		☐	☐	☐	☐
		☐	☐	☐	☐
		☐	☐	☐	☐
		☐	☐	☐	☐
		☐	☐	☐	☐
		☐	☐	☐	☐
(D) TOTAL	$				

DEBT REPAYMENT

Record any payments in excess of the minimum payment due.

CREDITOR	PAYMENT	BALANCE
(E) TOTAL	$	

WEEK ONE SUMMARY

CATEGORY	AMOUNT
(A) Income Total	
(B) Bills & Expenses Total	-
(C) Cash Envelopes Total	-
(D) Savings/Sinking Funds Total	-
(E) Debt Repayment Total	-
NOTE: Subtract B/C/D/E from A to determine what's left. **What's Left**	=

WEEKLY SPENDING LOG

Use the Weekly Spending Log to determine what your current spending habits are. Review the log to assess and correct impulse spending.

DATE	TRANSACTION	AMOUNT	Planned/Budgeted	Impulse Purchase
			○	○
			○	○
			○	○
			○	○
			○	○
			○	○
			○	○
			○	○
			○	○
			○	○
			○	○
			○	○
			○	○
			○	○
			○	○
			○	○
			○	○
			○	○
			○	○
			○	○
			○	○
			○	○
			○	○
			○	○
			○	○
			○	○
			○	○
			○	○
			○	○
			○	○
	TOTAL	$		

Spending *Plan*

Week of:

INCOME		Salary/Wages	Investment	Business	Side-Hustle
INCOME SOURCE	AMOUNT				
Rollover from previous week		☐	☐	☐	☐
		☐	☐	☐	☐
		☐	☐	☐	☐
		☐	☐	☐	☐
		☐	☐	☐	☐
		☐	☐	☐	☐
		☐	☐	☐	☐
(A) TOTAL	$				

BILLS & EXPENSES		Cash	Credit Card	Debit	Check
PAY TO	AMOUNT				
		☐	☐	☐	☐
		☐	☐	☐	☐
		☐	☐	☐	☐
		☐	☐	☐	☐
		☐	☐	☐	☐
		☐	☐	☐	☐
		☐	☐	☐	☐
		☐	☐	☐	☐
		☐	☐	☐	☐
		☐	☐	☐	☐
		☐	☐	☐	☐
		☐	☐	☐	☐
		☐	☐	☐	☐
		☐	☐	☐	☐
		☐	☐	☐	☐
(B) TOTAL	$				

Financial Priorities

This week's financial goal(s)

CASH ENVELOPES							
CATEGORY	AMOUNT	BANKING WITHDRAWAL DENOMINATIONS					
		$1	$5	$10	$20	$50	$100
		DENOMINATION TOTAL					
(C) TOTAL	$						

SAVINGS/SINKING FUNDS

ACCOUNT	AMOUNT	Sinking Fund	Short Term	Long Term	Retirement
		☐	☐	☐	☐
		☐	☐	☐	☐
		☐	☐	☐	☐
		☐	☐	☐	☐
		☐	☐	☐	☐
		☐	☐	☐	☐
		☐	☐	☐	☐
		☐	☐	☐	☐
		☐	☐	☐	☐
		☐	☐	☐	☐
(D) TOTAL	$				

DEBT REPAYMENT

Record any payments in excess of the minimum payment due.

CREDITOR	PAYMENT	BALANCE
(E) TOTAL	$	

WEEK TWO SUMMARY

CATEGORY	AMOUNT
(A) Income Total	
(B) Bills & Expenses Total	-
(C) Cash Envelopes Total	-
(D) Savings/Sinking Funds Total	-
(E) Debt Repayment Total	-
NOTE: Subtract B/C/D/E from A to determine what's left. **What's Left**	=

WEEKLY SPENDING LOG

Use the Weekly Spending Log to determine what your current spending habits are. Review the log to assess and correct impulse spending.

DATE	TRANSACTION	AMOUNT	Planned/Budgeted	Impulse Purchase
			○	○
			○	○
			○	○
			○	○
			○	○
			○	○
			○	○
			○	○
			○	○
			○	○
			○	○
			○	○
			○	○
			○	○
			○	○
			○	○
			○	○
			○	○
			○	○
			○	○
			○	○
			○	○
			○	○
			○	○
			○	○
			○	○
			○	○
			○	○
			○	○
			○	○
	TOTAL	$		

Spending *Plan*

Week of:

INCOME		Salary/Wages	Investment	Business	Side-Hustle
INCOME SOURCE	AMOUNT				
Rollover from previous week		☐	☐	☐	☐
		☐	☐	☐	☐
		☐	☐	☐	☐
		☐	☐	☐	☐
		☐	☐	☐	☐
		☐	☐	☐	☐
		☐	☐	☐	☐
(A) TOTAL	$				

BILLS & EXPENSES		Cash	Credit Card	Debit	Check
PAY TO	AMOUNT				
		☐	☐	☐	☐
		☐	☐	☐	☐
		☐	☐	☐	☐
		☐	☐	☐	☐
		☐	☐	☐	☐
		☐	☐	☐	☐
		☐	☐	☐	☐
		☐	☐	☐	☐
		☐	☐	☐	☐
		☐	☐	☐	☐
		☐	☐	☐	☐
		☐	☐	☐	☐
		☐	☐	☐	☐
		☐	☐	☐	☐
		☐	☐	☐	☐
(B) TOTAL	$				

Financial Priorities

This week's financial goal(s)

CASH ENVELOPES							
CATEGORY	AMOUNT	BANKING WITHDRAWAL DENOMINATIONS					
		$1	$5	$10	$20	$50	$100
		DENOMINATION TOTAL					
(C) TOTAL	$						

SAVINGS/SINKING FUNDS

ACCOUNT	AMOUNT	Sinking Fund	Short Term	Long Term	Retirement
		☐	☐	☐	☐
		☐	☐	☐	☐
		☐	☐	☐	☐
		☐	☐	☐	☐
		☐	☐	☐	☐
		☐	☐	☐	☐
		☐	☐	☐	☐
		☐	☐	☐	☐
		☐	☐	☐	☐
		☐	☐	☐	☐
(D) TOTAL	$				

DEBT REPAYMENT

Record any payments in excess of the minimum payment due.

CREDITOR	PAYMENT	BALANCE
(E) TOTAL	$	

WEEK THREE SUMMARY

CATEGORY	AMOUNT
(A) Income Total	
(B) Bills & Expenses Total	-
(C) Cash Envelopes Total	-
(D) Savings/Sinking Funds Total	-
(E) Debt Repayment Total	-
NOTE: Subtract B/C/D/E from A to determine what's left. **What's Left**	=

WEEKLY SPENDING LOG

Use the Weekly Spending Log to determine what your current spending habits are. Review the log to assess and correct impulse spending.

DATE	TRANSACTION	AMOUNT	Planned/Budgeted	Impulse Purchase
			○	○
			○	○
			○	○
			○	○
			○	○
			○	○
			○	○
			○	○
			○	○
			○	○
			○	○
			○	○
			○	○
			○	○
			○	○
			○	○
			○	○
			○	○
			○	○
			○	○
			○	○
			○	○
			○	○
			○	○
			○	○
			○	○
			○	○
			○	○
			○	○
			○	○
			○	○
	TOTAL	$		

Spending *Plan*

Week of:

INCOME		Salary/Wages	Investment	Business	Side-Hustle
INCOME SOURCE	AMOUNT				
Rollover from previous week		☐	☐	☐	☐
		☐	☐	☐	☐
		☐	☐	☐	☐
		☐	☐	☐	☐
		☐	☐	☐	☐
		☐	☐	☐	☐
		☐	☐	☐	☐
(A) TOTAL	$				

BILLS & EXPENSES		Cash	Credit Card	Debit	Check
PAY TO	AMOUNT				
		☐	☐	☐	☐
		☐	☐	☐	☐
		☐	☐	☐	☐
		☐	☐	☐	☐
		☐	☐	☐	☐
		☐	☐	☐	☐
		☐	☐	☐	☐
		☐	☐	☐	☐
		☐	☐	☐	☐
		☐	☐	☐	☐
		☐	☐	☐	☐
		☐	☐	☐	☐
		☐	☐	☐	☐
		☐	☐	☐	☐
		☐	☐	☐	☐
(B) TOTAL	$				

Financial Priorities

This week's financial goal(s)

CASH ENVELOPES							
CATEGORY	AMOUNT	BANKING WITHDRAWAL DENOMINATIONS					
		$1	$5	$10	$20	$50	$100
		DENOMINATION TOTAL					
(C) TOTAL	$						

SAVINGS/SINKING FUNDS

ACCOUNT	AMOUNT	Sinking Fund	Short Term	Long Term	Retirement
		☐	☐	☐	☐
		☐	☐	☐	☐
		☐	☐	☐	☐
		☐	☐	☐	☐
		☐	☐	☐	☐
		☐	☐	☐	☐
		☐	☐	☐	☐
		☐	☐	☐	☐
		☐	☐	☐	☐
		☐	☐	☐	☐
(D) TOTAL	$				

DEBT REPAYMENT

Record any payments in excess of the minimum payment due.

CREDITOR	PAYMENT	BALANCE
(E) TOTAL	$	

WEEK FOUR SUMMARY

CATEGORY	AMOUNT
(A) Income Total	
(B) Bills & Expenses Total	-
(C) Cash Envelopes Total	-
(D) Savings/Sinking Funds Total	-
(E) Debt Repayment Total	-
NOTE: Subtract B/C/D/E from A to determine what's left. **What's Left**	=

WEEKLY SPENDING LOG

Use the Weekly Spending Log to determine what your current spending habits are. Review the log to assess and correct impulse spending.

DATE	TRANSACTION	AMOUNT	Planned/Budgeted	Impulse Purchase
			○	○
			○	○
			○	○
			○	○
			○	○
			○	○
			○	○
			○	○
			○	○
			○	○
			○	○
			○	○
			○	○
			○	○
			○	○
			○	○
			○	○
			○	○
			○	○
			○	○
			○	○
			○	○
			○	○
			○	○
			○	○
			○	○
			○	○
			○	○
			○	○
			○	○
	TOTAL	$		

Spending *Plan*

Week of:

INCOME					
INCOME SOURCE	AMOUNT	Salary/Wages	Investment	Business	Side-Hustle
Rollover from previous week		☐	☐	☐	☐
		☐	☐	☐	☐
		☐	☐	☐	☐
		☐	☐	☐	☐
		☐	☐	☐	☐
		☐	☐	☐	☐
		☐	☐	☐	☐
(A) TOTAL	$				

BILLS & EXPENSES					
PAY TO	AMOUNT	Cash	Credit Card	Debit	Check
		☐	☐	☐	☐
		☐	☐	☐	☐
		☐	☐	☐	☐
		☐	☐	☐	☐
		☐	☐	☐	☐
		☐	☐	☐	☐
		☐	☐	☐	☐
		☐	☐	☐	☐
		☐	☐	☐	☐
		☐	☐	☐	☐
		☐	☐	☐	☐
		☐	☐	☐	☐
		☐	☐	☐	☐
		☐	☐	☐	☐
		☐	☐	☐	☐
(B) TOTAL	$				

Financial Priorities

This week's financial goal(s)

CASH ENVELOPES							
CATEGORY	AMOUNT	BANKING WITHDRAWAL DENOMINATIONS					
		$1	$5	$10	$20	$50	$100
		DENOMINATION TOTAL					
(C) TOTAL	$						

SAVINGS/SINKING FUNDS

ACCOUNT	AMOUNT	Sinking Fund	Short Term	Long Term	Retirement
		☐	☐	☐	☐
		☐	☐	☐	☐
		☐	☐	☐	☐
		☐	☐	☐	☐
		☐	☐	☐	☐
		☐	☐	☐	☐
		☐	☐	☐	☐
		☐	☐	☐	☐
		☐	☐	☐	☐
		☐	☐	☐	☐
(D) TOTAL	$				

DEBT REPAYMENT

Record any payments in excess of the minimum payment due.

CREDITOR	PAYMENT	BALANCE
(E) TOTAL	$	

WEEK FIVE SUMMARY

CATEGORY	AMOUNT
(A) Income Total	
(B) Bills & Expenses Total	-
(C) Cash Envelopes Total	-
(D) Savings/Sinking Funds Total	-
(E) Debt Repayment Total	-
NOTE: Subtract B/C/D/E from A to determine what's left. **What's Left**	=

WEEKLY SPENDING LOG

Use the Weekly Spending Log to determine what your current spending habits are. Review the log to assess and correct impulse spending.

DATE	TRANSACTION	AMOUNT	Planned/Budgeted	Impulse Purchase
			○	○
			○	○
			○	○
			○	○
			○	○
			○	○
			○	○
			○	○
			○	○
			○	○
			○	○
			○	○
			○	○
			○	○
			○	○
			○	○
			○	○
			○	○
			○	○
			○	○
			○	○
			○	○
			○	○
			○	○
			○	○
			○	○
			○	○
			○	○
			○	○
			○	○
	TOTAL	$		

Monthly Spending *summary*

Income	
Week One	
Week Two	
Week Three	
Week Four	
Week Five	
(A) TOTAL	$

Bills and Expenses	
Week One	
Week Two	
Week Three	
Week Four	
Week Five	
(B) TOTAL	$

Cash Envelopes	
Week One	
Week Two	
Week Three	
Week Four	
Week Five	
(C) TOTAL	$

Savings/Sinking Funds	
Week One	
Week Two	
Week Three	
Week Four	
Week Five	
(D) TOTAL	$

Debt Repayment	
Week One	
Week Two	
Week Three	
Week Four	
Week Five	
(E) TOTAL	$

MONTHLY SUMMARY	
(A) Income Total	
(B) Bills & Expenses Total	-
(C) Cash Envelopes Total	-
(D) Savings/SF Total	-
(E) Debt Repayment Total	-
What's Left	=

Subtract B/C/D/E from A to determine what's left.

Spending Assessment

Are there expenditures in your spending plan that can be cut or reduced? If yes, list the details below.

Impulse Spending

Review the spending log for each week, then calculate the total amount of the transactions listed as impulse purchases.

$

notes/observations

30-Day No Spend *challenge*

JAN	FEB	MAR	APR	MAY	JUN	JUL	AUG	SEP	OCT	NOV	DEC

Place a check mark on the purse which corresponds to each day that you do not make an impulse or non-essential purchase.

Total number of no-spend days

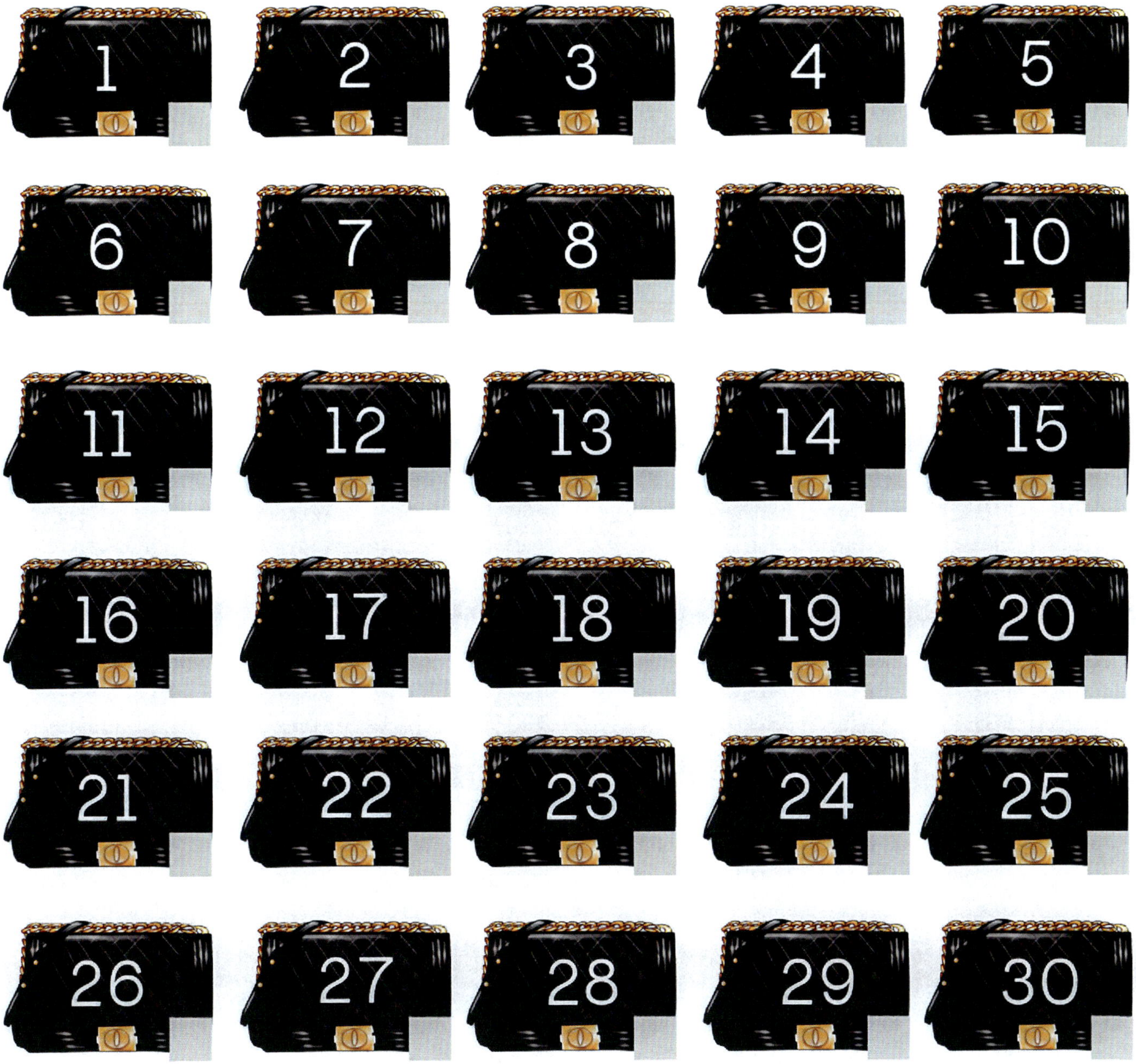

notes

Stay *focused*

"It's not how much money you make, but how much money you keep, how hard it works for you, and how many generations you keep it for."

MONTH TWO

Bill and Income *calendar*

FINANCIAL GOALS

MONDAY	TUESDAY	WEDNESDAY

JAN FEB MAR APR MAY JUN JUL AUG SEP OCT NOV DEC

THURSDAY	FRIDAY	SATURDAY	SUNDAY

Spending *Plan*

Week of:

Financial Priorities

This week's financial goal(s)

INCOME		Salary/Wages	Investment	Business	Side-Hustle
INCOME SOURCE	AMOUNT				
Rollover from previous week		☐	☐	☐	☐
		☐	☐	☐	☐
		☐	☐	☐	☐
		☐	☐	☐	☐
		☐	☐	☐	☐
		☐	☐	☐	☐
		☐	☐	☐	☐
(A) TOTAL	$				

BILLS & EXPENSES		Cash	Credit Card	Debit	Check
PAY TO	AMOUNT				
		☐	☐	☐	☐
		☐	☐	☐	☐
		☐	☐	☐	☐
		☐	☐	☐	☐
		☐	☐	☐	☐
		☐	☐	☐	☐
		☐	☐	☐	☐
		☐	☐	☐	☐
		☐	☐	☐	☐
		☐	☐	☐	☐
		☐	☐	☐	☐
		☐	☐	☐	☐
		☐	☐	☐	☐
		☐	☐	☐	☐
		☐	☐	☐	☐
(B) TOTAL	$				

CASH ENVELOPES							
CATEGORY	AMOUNT	BANKING WITHDRAWAL DENOMINATIONS					
		$1	$5	$10	$20	$50	$100
		DENOMINATION TOTAL					
(C) TOTAL	$						

SAVINGS/SINKING FUNDS

ACCOUNT	AMOUNT	Sinking Fund	Short Term	Long Term	Retirement
		☐	☐	☐	☐
		☐	☐	☐	☐
		☐	☐	☐	☐
		☐	☐	☐	☐
		☐	☐	☐	☐
		☐	☐	☐	☐
		☐	☐	☐	☐
		☐	☐	☐	☐
		☐	☐	☐	☐
		☐	☐	☐	☐
(D) TOTAL	$				

DEBT REPAYMENT

Record any payments in excess of the minimum payment due.

CREDITOR	PAYMENT	BALANCE
(E) TOTAL	$	

WEEK ONE SUMMARY

CATEGORY	AMOUNT
(A) Income Total	
(B) Bills & Expenses Total	-
(C) Cash Envelopes Total	-
(D) Savings/Sinking Funds Total	-
(E) Debt Repayment Total	-
NOTE: Subtract B/C/D/E from A to determine what's left. **What's Left**	=

WEEKLY SPENDING LOG

Use the Weekly Spending Log to determine what your current spending habits are. Review the log to assess and correct impulse spending.

DATE	TRANSACTION	AMOUNT	Planned/Budgeted	Impulse Purchase
			○	○
			○	○
			○	○
			○	○
			○	○
			○	○
			○	○
			○	○
			○	○
			○	○
			○	○
			○	○
			○	○
			○	○
			○	○
			○	○
			○	○
			○	○
			○	○
			○	○
			○	○
			○	○
			○	○
			○	○
			○	○
			○	○
			○	○
			○	○
			○	○
			○	○
	TOTAL	$		

Spending *Plan*

Week of:

INCOME

INCOME SOURCE	AMOUNT	Salary/Wages	Investment	Business	Side-Hustle
Rollover from previous week		☐	☐	☐	☐
		☐	☐	☐	☐
		☐	☐	☐	☐
		☐	☐	☐	☐
		☐	☐	☐	☐
		☐	☐	☐	☐
		☐	☐	☐	☐
(A) TOTAL	$				

BILLS & EXPENSES

PAY TO	AMOUNT	Cash	Credit Card	Debit	Check
		☐	☐	☐	☐
		☐	☐	☐	☐
		☐	☐	☐	☐
		☐	☐	☐	☐
		☐	☐	☐	☐
		☐	☐	☐	☐
		☐	☐	☐	☐
		☐	☐	☐	☐
		☐	☐	☐	☐
		☐	☐	☐	☐
		☐	☐	☐	☐
		☐	☐	☐	☐
		☐	☐	☐	☐
		☐	☐	☐	☐
		☐	☐	☐	☐
(B) TOTAL	$				

Financial Priorities

This week's financial goal(s)

CASH ENVELOPES

CATEGORY	AMOUNT	BANKING WITHDRAWAL DENOMINATIONS					
		$1	$5	$10	$20	$50	$100
		DENOMINATION TOTAL					
(C) TOTAL	$						

SAVINGS/SINKING FUNDS

ACCOUNT	AMOUNT	Sinking Fund	Short Term	Long Term	Retirement
		☐	☐	☐	☐
		☐	☐	☐	☐
		☐	☐	☐	☐
		☐	☐	☐	☐
		☐	☐	☐	☐
		☐	☐	☐	☐
		☐	☐	☐	☐
		☐	☐	☐	☐
		☐	☐	☐	☐
		☐	☐	☐	☐
(D) TOTAL	$				

DEBT REPAYMENT

Record any payments in excess of the minimum payment due.

CREDITOR	PAYMENT	BALANCE
(E) TOTAL	$	

WEEK TWO SUMMARY

CATEGORY	AMOUNT
(A) Income Total	
(B) Bills & Expenses Total	-
(C) Cash Envelopes Total	-
(D) Savings/Sinking Funds Total	-
(E) Debt Repayment Total	-
NOTE: Subtract B/C/D/E from A to determine what's left. **What's Left**	=

WEEKLY SPENDING LOG

Use the Weekly Spending Log to determine what your current spending habits are. Review the log to assess and correct impulse spending.

DATE	TRANSACTION	AMOUNT	Planned/Budgeted	Impulse Purchase
			○	○
			○	○
			○	○
			○	○
			○	○
			○	○
			○	○
			○	○
			○	○
			○	○
			○	○
			○	○
			○	○
			○	○
			○	○
			○	○
			○	○
			○	○
			○	○
			○	○
			○	○
			○	○
			○	○
			○	○
			○	○
			○	○
			○	○
			○	○
			○	○
			○	○
	TOTAL	$		

Spending *Plan*

Week of:

INCOME		Salary/Wages	Investment	Business	Side-Hustle
INCOME SOURCE	AMOUNT				
Rollover from previous week		☐	☐	☐	☐
		☐	☐	☐	☐
		☐	☐	☐	☐
		☐	☐	☐	☐
		☐	☐	☐	☐
		☐	☐	☐	☐
		☐	☐	☐	☐
(A) TOTAL	$				

BILLS & EXPENSES		Cash	Credit Card	Debit	Check
PAY TO	AMOUNT				
		☐	☐	☐	☐
		☐	☐	☐	☐
		☐	☐	☐	☐
		☐	☐	☐	☐
		☐	☐	☐	☐
		☐	☐	☐	☐
		☐	☐	☐	☐
		☐	☐	☐	☐
		☐	☐	☐	☐
		☐	☐	☐	☐
		☐	☐	☐	☐
		☐	☐	☐	☐
		☐	☐	☐	☐
		☐	☐	☐	☐
		☐	☐	☐	☐
(B) TOTAL	$				

Financial Priorities

This week's financial goal(s)

CASH ENVELOPES							
CATEGORY	AMOUNT	BANKING WITHDRAWAL DENOMINATIONS					
		$1	$5	$10	$20	$50	$100
		DENOMINATION TOTAL					
(C) TOTAL	$						

SAVINGS/SINKING FUNDS

ACCOUNT	AMOUNT	Sinking Fund	Short Term	Long Term	Retirement
		☐	☐	☐	☐
		☐	☐	☐	☐
		☐	☐	☐	☐
		☐	☐	☐	☐
		☐	☐	☐	☐
		☐	☐	☐	☐
		☐	☐	☐	☐
		☐	☐	☐	☐
		☐	☐	☐	☐
		☐	☐	☐	☐
(D) TOTAL	$				

DEBT REPAYMENT

Record any payments in excess of the minimum payment due.

CREDITOR	PAYMENT	BALANCE
(E) TOTAL	$	

WEEK THREE SUMMARY

CATEGORY	AMOUNT
(A) Income Total	
(B) Bills & Expenses Total	-
(C) Cash Envelopes Total	-
(D) Savings/Sinking Funds Total	-
(E) Debt Repayment Total	-
NOTE: Subtract B/C/D/E from A to determine what's left. **What's Left**	=

WEEKLY SPENDING LOG

Use the Weekly Spending Log to determine what your current spending habits are. Review the log to assess and correct impulse spending.

DATE	TRANSACTION	AMOUNT	Planned/Budgeted	Impulse Purchase
			○	○
			○	○
			○	○
			○	○
			○	○
			○	○
			○	○
			○	○
			○	○
			○	○
			○	○
			○	○
			○	○
			○	○
			○	○
			○	○
			○	○
			○	○
			○	○
			○	○
			○	○
			○	○
			○	○
			○	○
			○	○
			○	○
			○	○
			○	○
			○	○
			○	○
	TOTAL	$		

Spending Plan

Week of:

INCOME		Salary/Wages	Investment	Business	Side-Hustle
INCOME SOURCE	AMOUNT				
Rollover from previous week		☐	☐	☐	☐
		☐	☐	☐	☐
		☐	☐	☐	☐
		☐	☐	☐	☐
		☐	☐	☐	☐
		☐	☐	☐	☐
		☐	☐	☐	☐
(A) TOTAL	$				

BILLS & EXPENSES		Cash	Credit Card	Debit	Check
PAY TO	AMOUNT				
		☐	☐	☐	☐
		☐	☐	☐	☐
		☐	☐	☐	☐
		☐	☐	☐	☐
		☐	☐	☐	☐
		☐	☐	☐	☐
		☐	☐	☐	☐
		☐	☐	☐	☐
		☐	☐	☐	☐
		☐	☐	☐	☐
		☐	☐	☐	☐
		☐	☐	☐	☐
		☐	☐	☐	☐
		☐	☐	☐	☐
		☐	☐	☐	☐
(B) TOTAL	$				

Financial Priorities

This week's financial goal(s)

CASH ENVELOPES							
CATEGORY	AMOUNT	BANKING WITHDRAWAL DENOMINATIONS					
		$1	$5	$10	$20	$50	$100
		DENOMINATION TOTAL					
(C) TOTAL	$						

SAVINGS/SINKING FUNDS

ACCOUNT	AMOUNT	Sinking Fund	Short Term	Long Term	Retirement
		☐	☐	☐	☐
		☐	☐	☐	☐
		☐	☐	☐	☐
		☐	☐	☐	☐
		☐	☐	☐	☐
		☐	☐	☐	☐
		☐	☐	☐	☐
		☐	☐	☐	☐
		☐	☐	☐	☐
		☐	☐	☐	☐
(D) TOTAL	$				

DEBT REPAYMENT

Record any payments in excess of the minimum payment due.

CREDITOR	PAYMENT	BALANCE
(E) TOTAL	$	

WEEK FOUR SUMMARY

CATEGORY	AMOUNT
(A) Income Total	
(B) Bills & Expenses Total	-
(C) Cash Envelopes Total	-
(D) Savings/Sinking Funds Total	-
(E) Debt Repayment Total	-
NOTE: Subtract B/C/D/E from A to determine what's left. **What's Left**	=

WEEKLY SPENDING LOG

Use the Weekly Spending Log to determine what your current spending habits are. Review the log to assess and correct impulse spending.

DATE	TRANSACTION	AMOUNT	Planned/Budgeted	Impulse Purchase
			○	○
			○	○
			○	○
			○	○
			○	○
			○	○
			○	○
			○	○
			○	○
			○	○
			○	○
			○	○
			○	○
			○	○
			○	○
			○	○
			○	○
			○	○
			○	○
			○	○
			○	○
			○	○
			○	○
			○	○
			○	○
			○	○
			○	○
			○	○
			○	○
			○	○
	TOTAL	$		

Spending *Plan*

Week of:

INCOME		Salary/Wages	Investment	Business	Side-Hustle
INCOME SOURCE	AMOUNT				
Rollover from previous week		☐	☐	☐	☐
		☐	☐	☐	☐
		☐	☐	☐	☐
		☐	☐	☐	☐
		☐	☐	☐	☐
		☐	☐	☐	☐
		☐	☐	☐	☐
(A) TOTAL	$				

BILLS & EXPENSES		Cash	Credit Card	Debit	Check
PAY TO	AMOUNT				
		☐	☐	☐	☐
		☐	☐	☐	☐
		☐	☐	☐	☐
		☐	☐	☐	☐
		☐	☐	☐	☐
		☐	☐	☐	☐
		☐	☐	☐	☐
		☐	☐	☐	☐
		☐	☐	☐	☐
		☐	☐	☐	☐
		☐	☐	☐	☐
		☐	☐	☐	☐
		☐	☐	☐	☐
		☐	☐	☐	☐
		☐	☐	☐	☐
(B) TOTAL	$				

Financial Priorities

This week's financial goal(s)

CASH ENVELOPES							
CATEGORY	AMOUNT	BANKING WITHDRAWAL DENOMINATIONS					
		$1	$5	$10	$20	$50	$100
		DENOMINATION TOTAL					
(C) TOTAL	$						

SAVINGS/SINKING FUNDS

ACCOUNT	AMOUNT	Sinking Fund	Short Term	Long Term	Retirement
		☐	☐	☐	☐
		☐	☐	☐	☐
		☐	☐	☐	☐
		☐	☐	☐	☐
		☐	☐	☐	☐
		☐	☐	☐	☐
		☐	☐	☐	☐
		☐	☐	☐	☐
		☐	☐	☐	☐
		☐	☐	☐	☐
(D) TOTAL	$				

DEBT REPAYMENT

Record any payments in excess of the minimum payment due.

CREDITOR	PAYMENT	BALANCE
(E) TOTAL	$	

WEEK FIVE SUMMARY

CATEGORY	AMOUNT
(A) Income Total	
(B) Bills & Expenses Total	-
(C) Cash Envelopes Total	-
(D) Savings/Sinking Funds Total	-
(E) Debt Repayment Total	-
NOTE: Subtract B/C/D/E from A to determine what's left. **What's Left**	=

WEEKLY SPENDING LOG

Use the Weekly Spending Log to determine what your current spending habits are. Review the log to assess and correct impulse spending.

DATE	TRANSACTION	AMOUNT	Planned/Budgeted	Impulse Purchase
			○	○
			○	○
			○	○
			○	○
			○	○
			○	○
			○	○
			○	○
			○	○
			○	○
			○	○
			○	○
			○	○
			○	○
			○	○
			○	○
			○	○
			○	○
			○	○
			○	○
			○	○
			○	○
			○	○
			○	○
			○	○
			○	○
			○	○
			○	○
			○	○
			○	○
	TOTAL	$		

Monthly Spending *summary*

Income	
Week One	
Week Two	
Week Three	
Week Four	
Week Five	
(A) TOTAL	$

Bills and Expenses	
Week One	
Week Two	
Week Three	
Week Four	
Week Five	
(B) TOTAL	$

Cash Envelopes	
Week One	
Week Two	
Week Three	
Week Four	
Week Five	
(C) TOTAL	$

Savings/Sinking Funds	
Week One	
Week Two	
Week Three	
Week Four	
Week Five	
(D) TOTAL	$

Debt Repayment	
Week One	
Week Two	
Week Three	
Week Four	
Week Five	
(E) TOTAL	$

MONTHLY SUMMARY	
(A) Income Total	
(B) Bills & Expenses Total	-
(C) Cash Envelopes Total	-
(D) Savings/SF Total	-
(E) Debt Repayment Total	-
What's Left	=

Subtract B/C/D/E from A to determine what's left.

Spending Assessment

Are there expenditures in your spending plan that can be cut or reduced? If yes, list the details below.

Impulse Spending

Review the spending log for each week, then calculate the total amount of the transactions listed as impulse purchases.

$

notes/observations

30-Day No Spend *challenge*

JAN	FEB	MAR	APR	MAY	JUN	JUL	AUG	SEP	OCT	NOV	DEC

Place a check mark on the purse which corresponds to each day that you do not make an impulse or non-essential purchase.

Total number of no-spend days

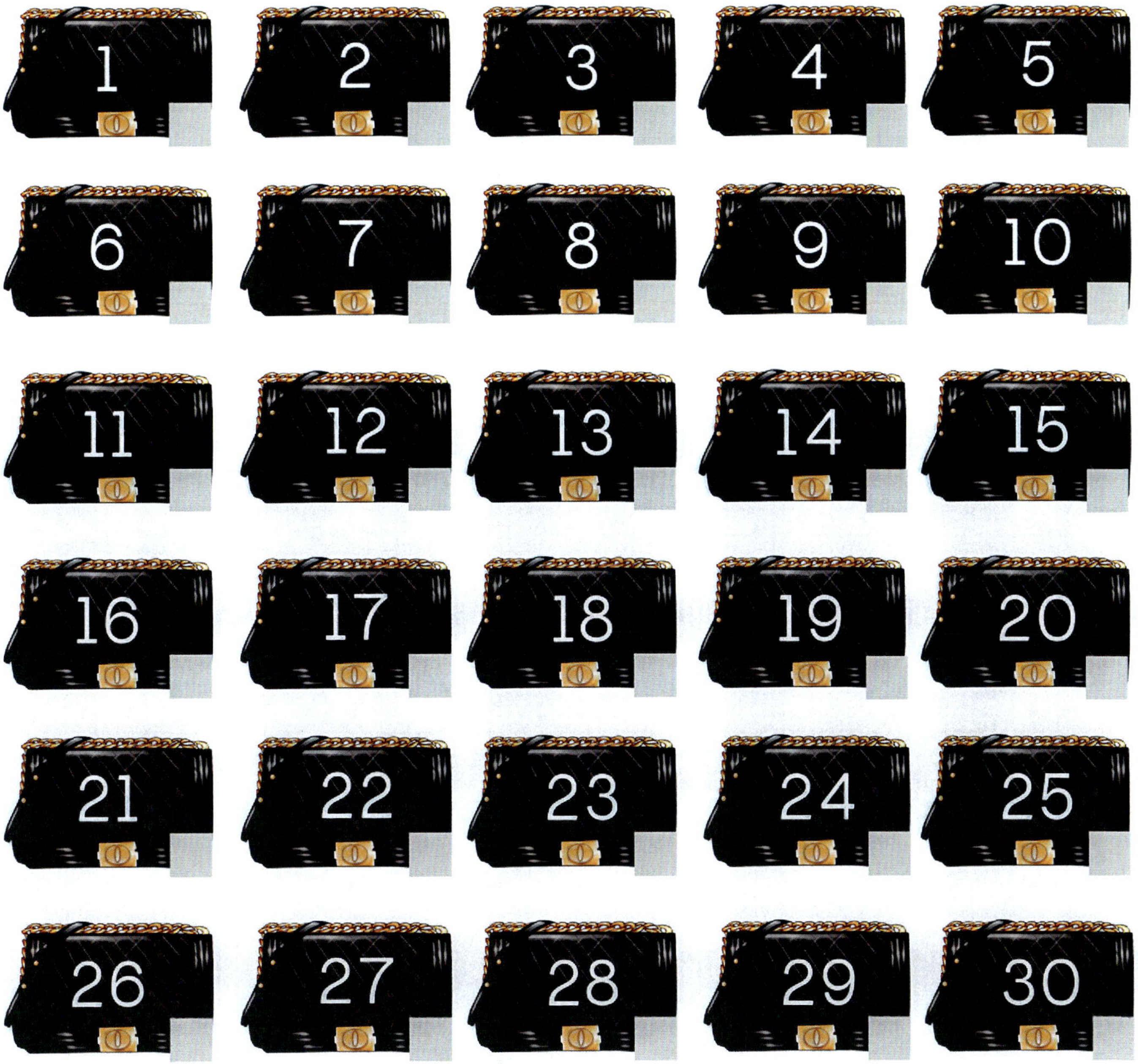

notes

Stay *focused*

"It's not how much money you make, but how much money you keep, how hard it works for you, and how many generations you keep it for."

MONTH THREE

Bill and Income *calendar*

FINANCIAL GOALS

MONDAY	TUESDAY	WEDNESDAY

JAN FEB MAR APR MAY JUN JUL AUG SEP OCT NOV DEC

THURSDAY	FRIDAY	SATURDAY	SUNDAY

Spending *Plan*

Week of:

Financial Priorities

This week's financial goal(s)

INCOME

INCOME SOURCE	AMOUNT	Salary/Wages	Investment	Business	Side-Hustle
Rollover from previous week		☐	☐	☐	☐
		☐	☐	☐	☐
		☐	☐	☐	☐
		☐	☐	☐	☐
		☐	☐	☐	☐
		☐	☐	☐	☐
		☐	☐	☐	☐
(A) TOTAL	$				

BILLS & EXPENSES

PAY TO	AMOUNT	Cash	Credit Card	Debit	Check
		☐	☐	☐	☐
		☐	☐	☐	☐
		☐	☐	☐	☐
		☐	☐	☐	☐
		☐	☐	☐	☐
		☐	☐	☐	☐
		☐	☐	☐	☐
		☐	☐	☐	☐
		☐	☐	☐	☐
		☐	☐	☐	☐
		☐	☐	☐	☐
		☐	☐	☐	☐
		☐	☐	☐	☐
		☐	☐	☐	☐
		☐	☐	☐	☐
(B) TOTAL	$				

CASH ENVELOPES

CATEGORY	AMOUNT	BANKING WITHDRAWAL DENOMINATIONS					
		$1	$5	$10	$20	$50	$100
		DENOMINATION TOTAL					
(C) TOTAL	$						

SAVINGS/SINKING FUNDS

ACCOUNT	AMOUNT	Sinking Fund	Short Term	Long Term	Retirement
		☐	☐	☐	☐
		☐	☐	☐	☐
		☐	☐	☐	☐
		☐	☐	☐	☐
		☐	☐	☐	☐
		☐	☐	☐	☐
		☐	☐	☐	☐
		☐	☐	☐	☐
		☐	☐	☐	☐
		☐	☐	☐	☐
(D) TOTAL	$				

DEBT REPAYMENT

Record any payments in excess of the minimum payment due.

CREDITOR	PAYMENT	BALANCE
(E) TOTAL	$	

WEEK ONE SUMMARY

CATEGORY	AMOUNT
(A) Income Total	
(B) Bills & Expenses Total	-
(C) Cash Envelopes Total	-
(D) Savings/Sinking Funds Total	-
(E) Debt Repayment Total	-
NOTE: Subtract B/C/D/E from A to determine what's left. **What's Left**	=

WEEKLY SPENDING LOG

Use the Weekly Spending Log to determine what your current spending habits are. Review the log to assess and correct impulse spending.

DATE	TRANSACTION	AMOUNT	Planned/Budgeted	Impulse Purchase
			○	○
			○	○
			○	○
			○	○
			○	○
			○	○
			○	○
			○	○
			○	○
			○	○
			○	○
			○	○
			○	○
			○	○
			○	○
			○	○
			○	○
			○	○
			○	○
			○	○
			○	○
			○	○
			○	○
			○	○
			○	○
			○	○
			○	○
			○	○
			○	○
			○	○
	TOTAL	$		

Spending *Plan*

Week of:

INCOME		Salary/Wages	Investment	Business	Side-Hustle
INCOME SOURCE	AMOUNT				
Rollover from previous week		☐	☐	☐	☐
		☐	☐	☐	☐
		☐	☐	☐	☐
		☐	☐	☐	☐
		☐	☐	☐	☐
		☐	☐	☐	☐
		☐	☐	☐	☐
(A) TOTAL	$				

BILLS & EXPENSES		Cash	Credit Card	Debit	Check
PAY TO	AMOUNT				
		☐	☐	☐	☐
		☐	☐	☐	☐
		☐	☐	☐	☐
		☐	☐	☐	☐
		☐	☐	☐	☐
		☐	☐	☐	☐
		☐	☐	☐	☐
		☐	☐	☐	☐
		☐	☐	☐	☐
		☐	☐	☐	☐
		☐	☐	☐	☐
		☐	☐	☐	☐
		☐	☐	☐	☐
		☐	☐	☐	☐
		☐	☐	☐	☐
(B) TOTAL	$				

Financial Priorities

This week's financial goal(s)

CASH ENVELOPES							
CATEGORY	AMOUNT	BANKING WITHDRAWAL DENOMINATIONS					
		$1	$5	$10	$20	$50	$100
		DENOMINATION TOTAL					
(C) TOTAL	$						

SAVINGS/SINKING FUNDS

ACCOUNT	AMOUNT	Sinking Fund	Short Term	Long Term	Retirement
		☐	☐	☐	☐
		☐	☐	☐	☐
		☐	☐	☐	☐
		☐	☐	☐	☐
		☐	☐	☐	☐
		☐	☐	☐	☐
		☐	☐	☐	☐
		☐	☐	☐	☐
		☐	☐	☐	☐
		☐	☐	☐	☐
(D) TOTAL	$				

DEBT REPAYMENT

Record any payments in excess of the minimum payment due.

CREDITOR	PAYMENT	BALANCE
(E) TOTAL	$	

WEEK TWO SUMMARY

CATEGORY	AMOUNT
(A) Income Total	
(B) Bills & Expenses Total	-
(C) Cash Envelopes Total	-
(D) Savings/Sinking Funds Total	-
(E) Debt Repayment Total	-
NOTE: Subtract B/C/D/E from A to determine what's left. **What's Left**	=

WEEKLY SPENDING LOG

Use the Weekly Spending Log to determine what your current spending habits are. Review the log to assess and correct impulse spending.

DATE	TRANSACTION	AMOUNT	Planned/Budgeted	Impulse Purchase
			○	○
			○	○
			○	○
			○	○
			○	○
			○	○
			○	○
			○	○
			○	○
			○	○
			○	○
			○	○
			○	○
			○	○
			○	○
			○	○
			○	○
			○	○
			○	○
			○	○
			○	○
			○	○
			○	○
			○	○
			○	○
			○	○
			○	○
			○	○
			○	○
			○	○
	TOTAL	$		

Spending *Plan*

Week of:

INCOME		Salary/Wages	Investment	Business	Side-Hustle
INCOME SOURCE	AMOUNT				
Rollover from previous week		☐	☐	☐	☐
		☐	☐	☐	☐
		☐	☐	☐	☐
		☐	☐	☐	☐
		☐	☐	☐	☐
		☐	☐	☐	☐
		☐	☐	☐	☐
(A) TOTAL	$				

BILLS & EXPENSES		Cash	Credit Card	Debit	Check
PAY TO	AMOUNT				
		☐	☐	☐	☐
		☐	☐	☐	☐
		☐	☐	☐	☐
		☐	☐	☐	☐
		☐	☐	☐	☐
		☐	☐	☐	☐
		☐	☐	☐	☐
		☐	☐	☐	☐
		☐	☐	☐	☐
		☐	☐	☐	☐
		☐	☐	☐	☐
		☐	☐	☐	☐
		☐	☐	☐	☐
		☐	☐	☐	☐
		☐	☐	☐	☐
(B) TOTAL	$				

Financial Priorities

This week's financial goal(s)

CASH ENVELOPES							
CATEGORY	AMOUNT	BANKING WITHDRAWAL DENOMINATIONS					
		$1	$5	$10	$20	$50	$100
		DENOMINATION TOTAL					
(C) TOTAL	$						

SAVINGS/SINKING FUNDS

ACCOUNT	AMOUNT	Sinking Fund	Short Term	Long Term	Retirement
		☐	☐	☐	☐
		☐	☐	☐	☐
		☐	☐	☐	☐
		☐	☐	☐	☐
		☐	☐	☐	☐
		☐	☐	☐	☐
		☐	☐	☐	☐
		☐	☐	☐	☐
		☐	☐	☐	☐
		☐	☐	☐	☐
(D) TOTAL	$				

DEBT REPAYMENT

Record any payments in excess of the minimum payment due.

CREDITOR	PAYMENT	BALANCE
(E) TOTAL	$	

WEEK THREE SUMMARY

CATEGORY	AMOUNT
(A) Income Total	
(B) Bills & Expenses Total	-
(C) Cash Envelopes Total	-
(D) Savings/Sinking Funds Total	-
(E) Debt Repayment Total	-
NOTE: Subtract B/C/D/E from A to determine what's left. **What's Left**	=

WEEKLY SPENDING LOG

Use the Weekly Spending Log to determine what your current spending habits are. Review the log to assess and correct impulse spending.

DATE	TRANSACTION	AMOUNT	Planned/Budgeted	Impulse Purchase
			○	○
			○	○
			○	○
			○	○
			○	○
			○	○
			○	○
			○	○
			○	○
			○	○
			○	○
			○	○
			○	○
			○	○
			○	○
			○	○
			○	○
			○	○
			○	○
			○	○
			○	○
			○	○
			○	○
			○	○
			○	○
			○	○
			○	○
			○	○
			○	○
			○	○
TOTAL		$		

Spending *Plan*

Week of:

INCOME		Salary/Wages	Investment	Business	Side-Hustle
INCOME SOURCE	AMOUNT				
Rollover from previous week		☐	☐	☐	☐
		☐	☐	☐	☐
		☐	☐	☐	☐
		☐	☐	☐	☐
		☐	☐	☐	☐
		☐	☐	☐	☐
		☐	☐	☐	☐
(A) TOTAL	$				

BILLS & EXPENSES		Cash	Credit Card	Debit	Check
PAY TO	AMOUNT				
		☐	☐	☐	☐
		☐	☐	☐	☐
		☐	☐	☐	☐
		☐	☐	☐	☐
		☐	☐	☐	☐
		☐	☐	☐	☐
		☐	☐	☐	☐
		☐	☐	☐	☐
		☐	☐	☐	☐
		☐	☐	☐	☐
		☐	☐	☐	☐
		☐	☐	☐	☐
		☐	☐	☐	☐
		☐	☐	☐	☐
		☐	☐	☐	☐
(B) TOTAL	$				

Financial Priorities

This week's financial goal(s)

CASH ENVELOPES							
CATEGORY	AMOUNT	BANKING WITHDRAWAL DENOMINATIONS					
		$1	$5	$10	$20	$50	$100
		DENOMINATION TOTAL					
(C) TOTAL	$						

SAVINGS/SINKING FUNDS

ACCOUNT	AMOUNT	Sinking Fund	Short Term	Long Term	Retirement
		☐	☐	☐	☐
		☐	☐	☐	☐
		☐	☐	☐	☐
		☐	☐	☐	☐
		☐	☐	☐	☐
		☐	☐	☐	☐
		☐	☐	☐	☐
		☐	☐	☐	☐
		☐	☐	☐	☐
		☐	☐	☐	☐
(D) TOTAL	$				

DEBT REPAYMENT

Record any payments in excess of the minimum payment due.

CREDITOR	PAYMENT	BALANCE
(E) TOTAL	$	

WEEK FOUR SUMMARY

CATEGORY	AMOUNT
(A) Income Total	
(B) Bills & Expenses Total	-
(C) Cash Envelopes Total	-
(D) Savings/Sinking Funds Total	-
(E) Debt Repayment Total	-
NOTE: Subtract B/C/D/E from A to determine what's left. **What's Left**	=

WEEKLY SPENDING LOG

Use the Weekly Spending Log to determine what your current spending habits are. Review the log to assess and correct impulse spending.

DATE	TRANSACTION	AMOUNT	Planned/Budgeted	Impulse Purchase
			○	○
			○	○
			○	○
			○	○
			○	○
			○	○
			○	○
			○	○
			○	○
			○	○
			○	○
			○	○
			○	○
			○	○
			○	○
			○	○
			○	○
			○	○
			○	○
			○	○
			○	○
			○	○
			○	○
			○	○
			○	○
			○	○
			○	○
			○	○
			○	○
			○	○
	TOTAL	$		

Spending *Plan*

Week of:

INCOME		Salary/Wages	Investment	Business	Side-Hustle
INCOME SOURCE	AMOUNT				
Rollover from previous week		☐	☐	☐	☐
		☐	☐	☐	☐
		☐	☐	☐	☐
		☐	☐	☐	☐
		☐	☐	☐	☐
		☐	☐	☐	☐
		☐	☐	☐	☐
(A) TOTAL	$				

BILLS & EXPENSES		Cash	Credit Card	Debit	Check
PAY TO	AMOUNT				
		☐	☐	☐	☐
		☐	☐	☐	☐
		☐	☐	☐	☐
		☐	☐	☐	☐
		☐	☐	☐	☐
		☐	☐	☐	☐
		☐	☐	☐	☐
		☐	☐	☐	☐
		☐	☐	☐	☐
		☐	☐	☐	☐
		☐	☐	☐	☐
		☐	☐	☐	☐
		☐	☐	☐	☐
		☐	☐	☐	☐
		☐	☐	☐	☐
(B) TOTAL	$				

Financial Priorities

This week's financial goal(s)

CASH ENVELOPES							
CATEGORY	AMOUNT	BANKING WITHDRAWAL DENOMINATIONS					
		$1	$5	$10	$20	$50	$100
		DENOMINATION TOTAL					
(C) TOTAL	$						

SAVINGS/SINKING FUNDS

ACCOUNT	AMOUNT	Sinking Fund	Short Term	Long Term	Retirement
		☐	☐	☐	☐
		☐	☐	☐	☐
		☐	☐	☐	☐
		☐	☐	☐	☐
		☐	☐	☐	☐
		☐	☐	☐	☐
		☐	☐	☐	☐
		☐	☐	☐	☐
		☐	☐	☐	☐
		☐	☐	☐	☐
(D) TOTAL	$				

DEBT REPAYMENT

Record any payments in excess of the minimum payment due.

CREDITOR	PAYMENT	BALANCE
(E) TOTAL	$	

WEEK FIVE SUMMARY

CATEGORY	AMOUNT
(A) Income Total	
(B) Bills & Expenses Total	-
(C) Cash Envelopes Total	-
(D) Savings/Sinking Funds Total	-
(E) Debt Repayment Total	-
NOTE: Subtract B/C/D/E from A to determine what's left. **What's Left**	=

WEEKLY SPENDING LOG

Use the Weekly Spending Log to determine what your current spending habits are. Review the log to assess and correct impulse spending.

DATE	TRANSACTION	AMOUNT	Planned/Budgeted	Impulse Purchase
			○	○
			○	○
			○	○
			○	○
			○	○
			○	○
			○	○
			○	○
			○	○
			○	○
			○	○
			○	○
			○	○
			○	○
			○	○
			○	○
			○	○
			○	○
			○	○
			○	○
			○	○
			○	○
			○	○
			○	○
			○	○
			○	○
			○	○
			○	○
			○	○
			○	○
	TOTAL	$		

Monthly Spending *summary*

Income	
Week One	
Week Two	
Week Three	
Week Four	
Week Five	
(A) TOTAL	$

Bills and Expenses	
Week One	
Week Two	
Week Three	
Week Four	
Week Five	
(B) TOTAL	$

Cash Envelopes	
Week One	
Week Two	
Week Three	
Week Four	
Week Five	
(C) TOTAL	$

Savings/Sinking Funds	
Week One	
Week Two	
Week Three	
Week Four	
Week Five	
(D) TOTAL	$

Debt Repayment	
Week One	
Week Two	
Week Three	
Week Four	
Week Five	
(E) TOTAL	$

MONTHLY SUMMARY	
(A) Income Total	
(B) Bills & Expenses Total	-
(C) Cash Envelopes Total	-
(D) Savings/SF Total	-
(E) Debt Repayment Total	-
What's Left	=

Subtract B/C/D/E from A to determine what's left.

Spending Assessment

Are there expenditures in your spending plan that can be cut or reduced? If yes, list the details below.

Impulse Spending

Review the spending log for each week, then calculate the total amount of the transactions listed as impulse purchases.

$

notes/observations

30-Day No Spend *challenge*

JAN	FEB	MAR	APR	MAY	JUN	JUL	AUG	SEP	OCT	NOV	DEC

Place a check mark on the purse which corresponds to each day that you do not make an impulse or non-essential purchase.

Total number of no-spend days

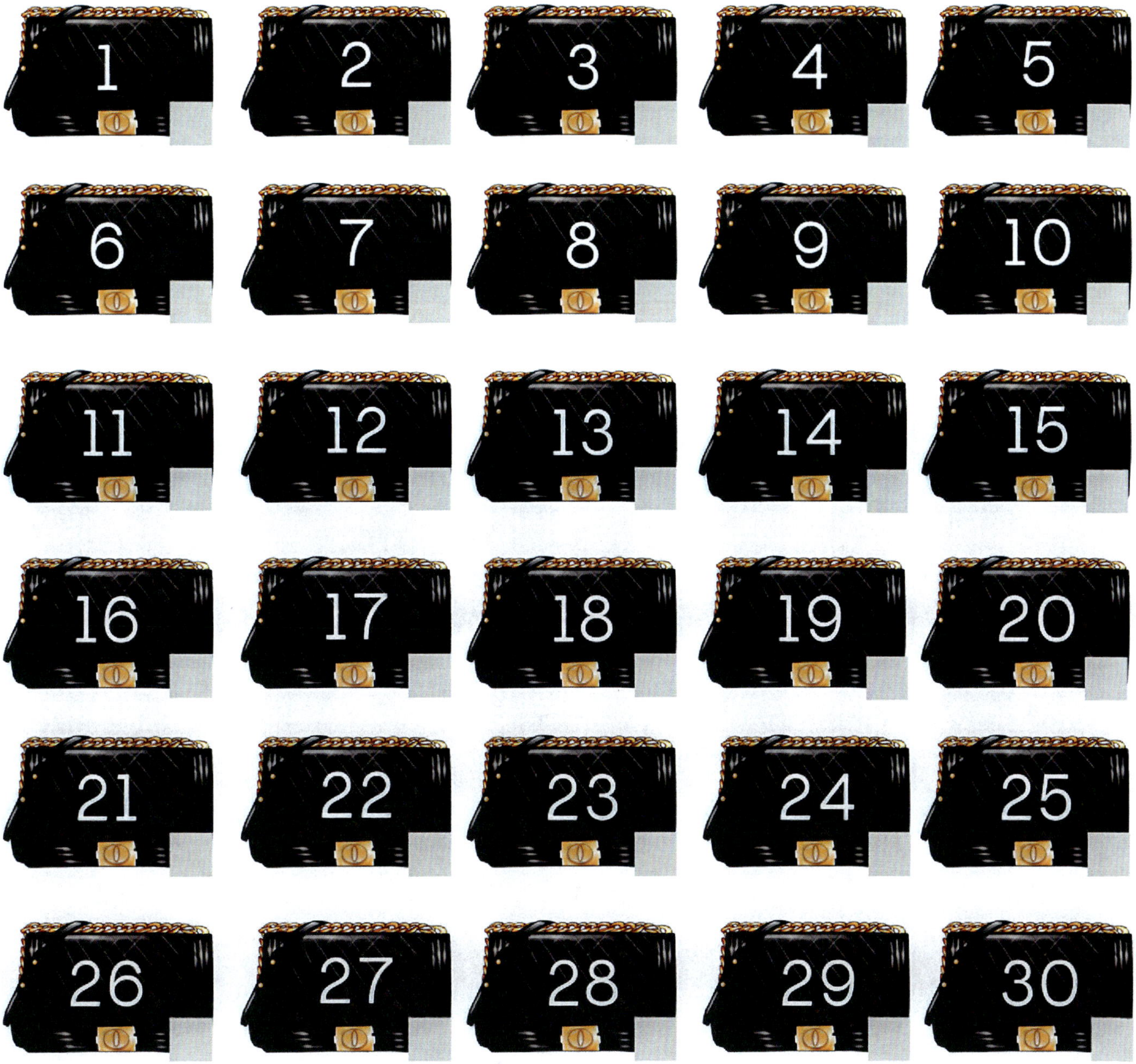

notes

Stay *focused*

"It's not how much money you make, but how much money you keep, how hard it works for you, and how many generations you keep it for."

MONTH FOUR

Bill and Income *calendar*

FINANCIAL GOALS

MONDAY	TUESDAY	WEDNESDAY

JAN FEB MAR APR MAY JUN JUL AUG SEP OCT NOV DEC

THURSDAY	FRIDAY	SATURDAY	SUNDAY

Spending *Plan*

Week of:

INCOME		Salary/Wages	Investment	Business	Side-Hustle
INCOME SOURCE	AMOUNT				
Rollover from previous week		☐	☐	☐	☐
		☐	☐	☐	☐
		☐	☐	☐	☐
		☐	☐	☐	☐
		☐	☐	☐	☐
		☐	☐	☐	☐
		☐	☐	☐	☐
(A) TOTAL	$				

BILLS & EXPENSES		Cash	Credit Card	Debit	Check
PAY TO	AMOUNT				
		☐	☐	☐	☐
		☐	☐	☐	☐
		☐	☐	☐	☐
		☐	☐	☐	☐
		☐	☐	☐	☐
		☐	☐	☐	☐
		☐	☐	☐	☐
		☐	☐	☐	☐
		☐	☐	☐	☐
		☐	☐	☐	☐
		☐	☐	☐	☐
		☐	☐	☐	☐
		☐	☐	☐	☐
		☐	☐	☐	☐
		☐	☐	☐	☐
(B) TOTAL	$				

Financial Priorities

This week's financial goal(s)

CASH ENVELOPES							
CATEGORY	AMOUNT	BANKING WITHDRAWAL DENOMINATIONS					
		$1	$5	$10	$20	$50	$100
		DENOMINATION TOTAL					
(C) TOTAL	$						

SAVINGS/SINKING FUNDS

ACCOUNT	AMOUNT	Sinking Fund	Short Term	Long Term	Retirement
		☐	☐	☐	☐
		☐	☐	☐	☐
		☐	☐	☐	☐
		☐	☐	☐	☐
		☐	☐	☐	☐
		☐	☐	☐	☐
		☐	☐	☐	☐
		☐	☐	☐	☐
		☐	☐	☐	☐
		☐	☐	☐	☐
(D) TOTAL	$				

DEBT REPAYMENT

Record any payments in excess of the minimum payment due.

CREDITOR	PAYMENT	BALANCE
(E) TOTAL	$	

WEEK ONE SUMMARY

CATEGORY	AMOUNT
(A) Income Total	
(B) Bills & Expenses Total	-
(C) Cash Envelopes Total	-
(D) Savings/Sinking Funds Total	-
(E) Debt Repayment Total	-
NOTE: Subtract B/C/D/E from A to determine what's left. **What's Left**	=

WEEKLY SPENDING LOG

Use the Weekly Spending Log to determine what your current spending habits are. Review the log to assess and correct impulse spending.

DATE	TRANSACTION	AMOUNT	Planned/Budgeted	Impulse Purchase
			○	○
			○	○
			○	○
			○	○
			○	○
			○	○
			○	○
			○	○
			○	○
			○	○
			○	○
			○	○
			○	○
			○	○
			○	○
			○	○
			○	○
			○	○
			○	○
			○	○
			○	○
			○	○
			○	○
			○	○
			○	○
			○	○
			○	○
			○	○
			○	○
			○	○
	TOTAL	$		

Spending *Plan*

Week of:

INCOME					
INCOME SOURCE	AMOUNT	Salary/Wages	Investment	Business	Side-Hustle
Rollover from previous week		☐	☐	☐	☐
		☐	☐	☐	☐
		☐	☐	☐	☐
		☐	☐	☐	☐
		☐	☐	☐	☐
		☐	☐	☐	☐
		☐	☐	☐	☐
(A) TOTAL	$				

BILLS & EXPENSES					
PAY TO	AMOUNT	Cash	Credit Card	Debit	Check
		☐	☐	☐	☐
		☐	☐	☐	☐
		☐	☐	☐	☐
		☐	☐	☐	☐
		☐	☐	☐	☐
		☐	☐	☐	☐
		☐	☐	☐	☐
		☐	☐	☐	☐
		☐	☐	☐	☐
		☐	☐	☐	☐
		☐	☐	☐	☐
		☐	☐	☐	☐
		☐	☐	☐	☐
		☐	☐	☐	☐
		☐	☐	☐	☐
(B) TOTAL	$				

Financial Priorities

This week's financial goal(s)

CASH ENVELOPES							
CATEGORY	AMOUNT	BANKING WITHDRAWAL DENOMINATIONS					
		$1	$5	$10	$20	$50	$100
		DENOMINATION TOTAL					
(C) TOTAL	$						

SAVINGS/SINKING FUNDS

ACCOUNT	AMOUNT	Sinking Fund	Short Term	Long Term	Retirement
		☐	☐	☐	☐
		☐	☐	☐	☐
		☐	☐	☐	☐
		☐	☐	☐	☐
		☐	☐	☐	☐
		☐	☐	☐	☐
		☐	☐	☐	☐
		☐	☐	☐	☐
		☐	☐	☐	☐
		☐	☐	☐	☐
(D) TOTAL	$				

DEBT REPAYMENT

Record any payments in excess of the minimum payment due.

CREDITOR	PAYMENT	BALANCE
(E) TOTAL	$	

WEEK TWO SUMMARY

CATEGORY	AMOUNT
(A) Income Total	
(B) Bills & Expenses Total	-
(C) Cash Envelopes Total	-
(D) Savings/Sinking Funds Total	-
(E) Debt Repayment Total	-
NOTE: Subtract B/C/D/E from A to determine what's left. **What's Left**	=

WEEKLY SPENDING LOG

Use the Weekly Spending Log to determine what your current spending habits are. Review the log to assess and correct impulse spending.

DATE	TRANSACTION	AMOUNT	Planned/Budgeted	Impulse Purchase
			○	○
			○	○
			○	○
			○	○
			○	○
			○	○
			○	○
			○	○
			○	○
			○	○
			○	○
			○	○
			○	○
			○	○
			○	○
			○	○
			○	○
			○	○
			○	○
			○	○
			○	○
			○	○
			○	○
			○	○
			○	○
			○	○
			○	○
			○	○
			○	○
			○	○
	TOTAL	$		

Spending *Plan*

Week of:

INCOME		Salary/Wages	Investment	Business	Side-Hustle
INCOME SOURCE	AMOUNT				
Rollover from previous week		☐	☐	☐	☐
		☐	☐	☐	☐
		☐	☐	☐	☐
		☐	☐	☐	☐
		☐	☐	☐	☐
		☐	☐	☐	☐
		☐	☐	☐	☐
(A) TOTAL	$				

BILLS & EXPENSES		Cash	Credit Card	Debit	Check
PAY TO	AMOUNT				
		☐	☐	☐	☐
		☐	☐	☐	☐
		☐	☐	☐	☐
		☐	☐	☐	☐
		☐	☐	☐	☐
		☐	☐	☐	☐
		☐	☐	☐	☐
		☐	☐	☐	☐
		☐	☐	☐	☐
		☐	☐	☐	☐
		☐	☐	☐	☐
		☐	☐	☐	☐
		☐	☐	☐	☐
		☐	☐	☐	☐
		☐	☐	☐	☐
(B) TOTAL	$				

Financial Priorities

This week's financial goal(s)

CASH ENVELOPES							
CATEGORY	AMOUNT	BANKING WITHDRAWAL DENOMINATIONS					
		$1	$5	$10	$20	$50	$100
		DENOMINATION TOTAL					
(C) TOTAL	$						

SAVINGS/SINKING FUNDS

ACCOUNT	AMOUNT	Sinking Fund	Short Term	Long Term	Retirement
		☐	☐	☐	☐
		☐	☐	☐	☐
		☐	☐	☐	☐
		☐	☐	☐	☐
		☐	☐	☐	☐
		☐	☐	☐	☐
		☐	☐	☐	☐
		☐	☐	☐	☐
		☐	☐	☐	☐
		☐	☐	☐	☐
(D) TOTAL	$				

DEBT REPAYMENT

Record any payments in excess of the minimum payment due.

CREDITOR	PAYMENT	BALANCE
(E) TOTAL	$	

WEEK THREE SUMMARY

CATEGORY	AMOUNT
(A) Income Total	
(B) Bills & Expenses Total	-
(C) Cash Envelopes Total	-
(D) Savings/Sinking Funds Total	-
(E) Debt Repayment Total	-
NOTE: Subtract B/C/D/E from A to determine what's left. **What's Left**	=

WEEKLY SPENDING LOG

Use the Weekly Spending Log to determine what your current spending habits are. Review the log to assess and correct impulse spending.

DATE	TRANSACTION	AMOUNT	Planned/Budgeted	Impulse Purchase
			○	○
			○	○
			○	○
			○	○
			○	○
			○	○
			○	○
			○	○
			○	○
			○	○
			○	○
			○	○
			○	○
			○	○
			○	○
			○	○
			○	○
			○	○
			○	○
			○	○
			○	○
			○	○
			○	○
			○	○
			○	○
			○	○
			○	○
			○	○
			○	○
			○	○
	TOTAL	$		

Spending *Plan*

Week of:

INCOME		Salary/Wages	Investment	Business	Side-Hustle
INCOME SOURCE	AMOUNT				
Rollover from previous week		☐	☐	☐	☐
		☐	☐	☐	☐
		☐	☐	☐	☐
		☐	☐	☐	☐
		☐	☐	☐	☐
		☐	☐	☐	☐
		☐	☐	☐	☐
(A) TOTAL	$				

BILLS & EXPENSES		Cash	Credit Card	Debit	Check
PAY TO	AMOUNT				
		☐	☐	☐	☐
		☐	☐	☐	☐
		☐	☐	☐	☐
		☐	☐	☐	☐
		☐	☐	☐	☐
		☐	☐	☐	☐
		☐	☐	☐	☐
		☐	☐	☐	☐
		☐	☐	☐	☐
		☐	☐	☐	☐
		☐	☐	☐	☐
		☐	☐	☐	☐
		☐	☐	☐	☐
		☐	☐	☐	☐
		☐	☐	☐	☐
(B) TOTAL	$				

Financial Priorities

This week's financial goal(s)

CASH ENVELOPES							
CATEGORY	AMOUNT	BANKING WITHDRAWAL DENOMINATIONS					
		$1	$5	$10	$20	$50	$100
		DENOMINATION TOTAL					
(C) TOTAL	$						

SAVINGS/SINKING FUNDS

ACCOUNT	AMOUNT	Sinking Fund	Short Term	Long Term	Retirement
		☐	☐	☐	☐
		☐	☐	☐	☐
		☐	☐	☐	☐
		☐	☐	☐	☐
		☐	☐	☐	☐
		☐	☐	☐	☐
		☐	☐	☐	☐
		☐	☐	☐	☐
		☐	☐	☐	☐
		☐	☐	☐	☐
(D) TOTAL	$				

DEBT REPAYMENT

Record any payments in excess of the minimum payment due.

CREDITOR	PAYMENT	BALANCE
(E) TOTAL	$	

WEEK FOUR SUMMARY

CATEGORY	AMOUNT
(A) Income Total	
(B) Bills & Expenses Total	-
(C) Cash Envelopes Total	-
(D) Savings/Sinking Funds Total	-
(E) Debt Repayment Total	-
NOTE: Subtract B/C/D/E from A to determine what's left. **What's Left**	=

WEEKLY SPENDING LOG

Use the Weekly Spending Log to determine what your current spending habits are. Review the log to assess and correct impulse spending.

DATE	TRANSACTION	AMOUNT	Planned/Budgeted	Impulse Purchase
			○	○
			○	○
			○	○
			○	○
			○	○
			○	○
			○	○
			○	○
			○	○
			○	○
			○	○
			○	○
			○	○
			○	○
			○	○
			○	○
			○	○
			○	○
			○	○
			○	○
			○	○
			○	○
			○	○
			○	○
			○	○
			○	○
			○	○
			○	○
			○	○
			○	○
	TOTAL	$		

Spending *Plan*

Week of:

Financial Priorities

This week's financial goal(s)

INCOME					
INCOME SOURCE	AMOUNT	Salary/Wages	Investment	Business	Side-Hustle
Rollover from previous week		☐	☐	☐	☐
		☐	☐	☐	☐
		☐	☐	☐	☐
		☐	☐	☐	☐
		☐	☐	☐	☐
		☐	☐	☐	☐
		☐	☐	☐	☐
(A) TOTAL	$				

BILLS & EXPENSES					
PAY TO	AMOUNT	Cash	Credit Card	Debit	Check
		☐	☐	☐	☐
		☐	☐	☐	☐
		☐	☐	☐	☐
		☐	☐	☐	☐
		☐	☐	☐	☐
		☐	☐	☐	☐
		☐	☐	☐	☐
		☐	☐	☐	☐
		☐	☐	☐	☐
		☐	☐	☐	☐
		☐	☐	☐	☐
		☐	☐	☐	☐
		☐	☐	☐	☐
		☐	☐	☐	☐
		☐	☐	☐	☐
(B) TOTAL	$				

CASH ENVELOPES								
CATEGORY	AMOUNT	BANKING WITHDRAWAL DENOMINATIONS						
		$1	$5	$10	$20	$50	$100	
		DENOMINATION TOTAL						
(C) TOTAL	$							

SAVINGS/SINKING FUNDS

ACCOUNT	AMOUNT	Sinking Fund	Short Term	Long Term	Retirement
		☐	☐	☐	☐
		☐	☐	☐	☐
		☐	☐	☐	☐
		☐	☐	☐	☐
		☐	☐	☐	☐
		☐	☐	☐	☐
		☐	☐	☐	☐
		☐	☐	☐	☐
		☐	☐	☐	☐
		☐	☐	☐	☐
(D) TOTAL	$				

DEBT REPAYMENT

Record any payments in excess of the minimum payment due.

CREDITOR	PAYMENT	BALANCE
(E) TOTAL	$	

WEEK FIVE SUMMARY

CATEGORY	AMOUNT
(A) Income Total	
(B) Bills & Expenses Total	-
(C) Cash Envelopes Total	-
(D) Savings/Sinking Funds Total	-
(E) Debt Repayment Total	-
NOTE: Subtract B/C/D/E from A to determine what's left. **What's Left**	=

WEEKLY SPENDING LOG

Use the Weekly Spending Log to determine what your current spending habits are. Review the log to assess and correct impulse spending.

DATE	TRANSACTION	AMOUNT	Planned/Budgeted	Impulse Purchase
			○	○
			○	○
			○	○
			○	○
			○	○
			○	○
			○	○
			○	○
			○	○
			○	○
			○	○
			○	○
			○	○
			○	○
			○	○
			○	○
			○	○
			○	○
			○	○
			○	○
			○	○
			○	○
			○	○
			○	○
			○	○
			○	○
			○	○
			○	○
			○	○
			○	○
	TOTAL	$		

Monthly Spending *summary*

Income	
Week One	
Week Two	
Week Three	
Week Four	
Week Five	
(A) TOTAL	$

Bills and Expenses	
Week One	
Week Two	
Week Three	
Week Four	
Week Five	
(B) TOTAL	$

Spending Assessment

Are there expenditures in your spending plan that can be cut or reduced? If yes, list the details below.

Cash Envelopes	
Week One	
Week Two	
Week Three	
Week Four	
Week Five	
(C) TOTAL	$

Savings/Sinking Funds	
Week One	
Week Two	
Week Three	
Week Four	
Week Five	
(D) TOTAL	$

Impulse Spending

Review the spending log for each week, then calculate the total amount of the transactions listed as impulse purchases.

$

Debt Repayment	
Week One	
Week Two	
Week Three	
Week Four	
Week Five	
(E) TOTAL	$

MONTHLY SUMMARY	
(A) Income Total	
(B) Bills & Expenses Total	-
(C) Cash Envelopes Total	-
(D) Savings/SF Total	-
(E) Debt Repayment Total	-
What's Left	=

Subtract B/C/D/E from A to determine what's left.

notes/observations

30-Day No Spend *challenge*

JAN FEB MAR APR MAY JUN JUL AUG SEP OCT NOV DEC

Place a check mark on the purse which corresponds to each day that you do not make an impulse or non-essential purchase.

Total number of no-spend days

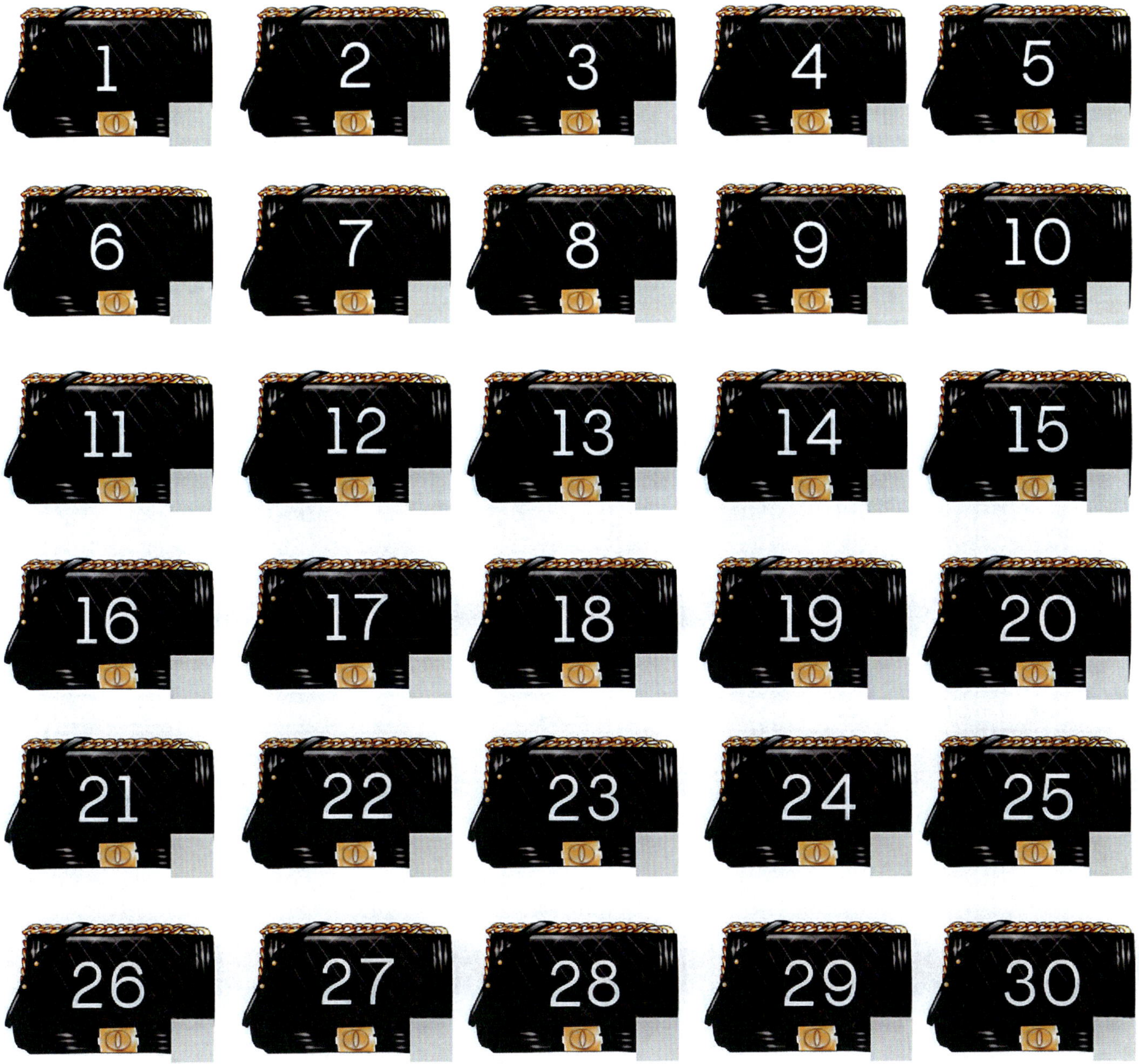

notes

Stay *focused*

"It's not how much money you make, but how much money you keep, how hard it works for you, and how many generations you keep it for."

MONTH FIVE

Bill and Income *calendar*

FINANCIAL GOALS

MONDAY	TUESDAY	WEDNESDAY

JAN FEB MAR APR MAY JUN JUL AUG SEP OCT NOV DEC

THURSDAY	FRIDAY	SATURDAY	SUNDAY

Spending *Plan*

Week of:

INCOME		Salary/Wages	Investment	Business	Side-Hustle
INCOME SOURCE	AMOUNT				
Rollover from previous week		☐	☐	☐	☐
		☐	☐	☐	☐
		☐	☐	☐	☐
		☐	☐	☐	☐
		☐	☐	☐	☐
		☐	☐	☐	☐
		☐	☐	☐	☐
(A) TOTAL	$				

BILLS & EXPENSES		Cash	Credit Card	Debit	Check
PAY TO	AMOUNT				
		☐	☐	☐	☐
		☐	☐	☐	☐
		☐	☐	☐	☐
		☐	☐	☐	☐
		☐	☐	☐	☐
		☐	☐	☐	☐
		☐	☐	☐	☐
		☐	☐	☐	☐
		☐	☐	☐	☐
		☐	☐	☐	☐
		☐	☐	☐	☐
		☐	☐	☐	☐
		☐	☐	☐	☐
		☐	☐	☐	☐
		☐	☐	☐	☐
(B) TOTAL	$				

Financial Priorities

This week's financial goal(s)

CASH ENVELOPES							
CATEGORY	AMOUNT	BANKING WITHDRAWAL DENOMINATIONS					
		$1	$5	$10	$20	$50	$100
		DENOMINATION TOTAL					
(C) TOTAL	$						

SAVINGS/SINKING FUNDS

ACCOUNT	AMOUNT	Sinking Fund	Short Term	Long Term	Retirement
		☐	☐	☐	☐
		☐	☐	☐	☐
		☐	☐	☐	☐
		☐	☐	☐	☐
		☐	☐	☐	☐
		☐	☐	☐	☐
		☐	☐	☐	☐
		☐	☐	☐	☐
		☐	☐	☐	☐
		☐	☐	☐	☐
(D) TOTAL	$				

DEBT REPAYMENT

Record any payments in excess of the minimum payment due.

CREDITOR	PAYMENT	BALANCE
(E) TOTAL	$	

WEEK ONE SUMMARY

CATEGORY	AMOUNT
(A) Income Total	
(B) Bills & Expenses Total	-
(C) Cash Envelopes Total	-
(D) Savings/Sinking Funds Total	-
(E) Debt Repayment Total	-
NOTE: Subtract B/C/D/E from A to determine what's left. **What's Left**	=

WEEKLY SPENDING LOG

Use the Weekly Spending Log to determine what your current spending habits are. Review the log to assess and correct impulse spending.

DATE	TRANSACTION	AMOUNT	Planned/Budgeted	Impulse Purchase
			○	○
			○	○
			○	○
			○	○
			○	○
			○	○
			○	○
			○	○
			○	○
			○	○
			○	○
			○	○
			○	○
			○	○
			○	○
			○	○
			○	○
			○	○
			○	○
			○	○
			○	○
			○	○
			○	○
			○	○
			○	○
			○	○
			○	○
			○	○
			○	○
			○	○
	TOTAL	$		

Spending *Plan*

Week of:

INCOME

INCOME SOURCE	AMOUNT	Salary/Wages	Investment	Business	Side-Hustle
Rollover from previous week		☐	☐	☐	☐
		☐	☐	☐	☐
		☐	☐	☐	☐
		☐	☐	☐	☐
		☐	☐	☐	☐
		☐	☐	☐	☐
		☐	☐	☐	☐
(A) TOTAL	$				

BILLS & EXPENSES

PAY TO	AMOUNT	Cash	Credit Card	Debit	Check
		☐	☐	☐	☐
		☐	☐	☐	☐
		☐	☐	☐	☐
		☐	☐	☐	☐
		☐	☐	☐	☐
		☐	☐	☐	☐
		☐	☐	☐	☐
		☐	☐	☐	☐
		☐	☐	☐	☐
		☐	☐	☐	☐
		☐	☐	☐	☐
		☐	☐	☐	☐
		☐	☐	☐	☐
		☐	☐	☐	☐
		☐	☐	☐	☐
(B) TOTAL	$				

Financial Priorities

This week's financial goal(s)

CASH ENVELOPES

CATEGORY	AMOUNT	BANKING WITHDRAWAL DENOMINATIONS					
		$1	$5	$10	$20	$50	$100
		DENOMINATION TOTAL					
(C) TOTAL	$						

SAVINGS/SINKING FUNDS

ACCOUNT	AMOUNT	Sinking Fund	Short Term	Long Term	Retirement
		☐	☐	☐	☐
		☐	☐	☐	☐
		☐	☐	☐	☐
		☐	☐	☐	☐
		☐	☐	☐	☐
		☐	☐	☐	☐
		☐	☐	☐	☐
		☐	☐	☐	☐
		☐	☐	☐	☐
		☐	☐	☐	☐
(D) TOTAL	$				

DEBT REPAYMENT

Record any payments in excess of the minimum payment due.

CREDITOR	PAYMENT	BALANCE
(E) TOTAL	$	

WEEK TWO SUMMARY

CATEGORY	AMOUNT
(A) Income Total	
(B) Bills & Expenses Total	-
(C) Cash Envelopes Total	-
(D) Savings/Sinking Funds Total	-
(E) Debt Repayment Total	-
NOTE: Subtract B/C/D/E from A to determine what's left. **What's Left**	=

WEEKLY SPENDING LOG

Use the Weekly Spending Log to determine what your current spending habits are. Review the log to assess and correct impulse spending.

DATE	TRANSACTION	AMOUNT	Planned/Budgeted	Impulse Purchase
			○	○
			○	○
			○	○
			○	○
			○	○
			○	○
			○	○
			○	○
			○	○
			○	○
			○	○
			○	○
			○	○
			○	○
			○	○
			○	○
			○	○
			○	○
			○	○
			○	○
			○	○
			○	○
			○	○
			○	○
			○	○
			○	○
			○	○
			○	○
			○	○
			○	○
	TOTAL	$		

Spending *Plan*

Week of:

Financial Priorities

This week's financial goal(s)

INCOME		Salary/Wages	Investment	Business	Side-Hustle
INCOME SOURCE	AMOUNT				
Rollover from previous week		☐	☐	☐	☐
		☐	☐	☐	☐
		☐	☐	☐	☐
		☐	☐	☐	☐
		☐	☐	☐	☐
		☐	☐	☐	☐
		☐	☐	☐	☐
(A) TOTAL	$				

BILLS & EXPENSES		Cash	Credit Card	Debit	Check
PAY TO	AMOUNT				
		☐	☐	☐	☐
		☐	☐	☐	☐
		☐	☐	☐	☐
		☐	☐	☐	☐
		☐	☐	☐	☐
		☐	☐	☐	☐
		☐	☐	☐	☐
		☐	☐	☐	☐
		☐	☐	☐	☐
		☐	☐	☐	☐
		☐	☐	☐	☐
		☐	☐	☐	☐
		☐	☐	☐	☐
		☐	☐	☐	☐
		☐	☐	☐	☐
(B) TOTAL	$				

CASH ENVELOPES							
CATEGORY	AMOUNT	BANKING WITHDRAWAL DENOMINATIONS					
		$1	$5	$10	$20	$50	$100
		DENOMINATION TOTAL					
(C) TOTAL	$						

SAVINGS/SINKING FUNDS

ACCOUNT	AMOUNT	Sinking Fund	Short Term	Long Term	Retirement
		☐	☐	☐	☐
		☐	☐	☐	☐
		☐	☐	☐	☐
		☐	☐	☐	☐
		☐	☐	☐	☐
		☐	☐	☐	☐
		☐	☐	☐	☐
		☐	☐	☐	☐
		☐	☐	☐	☐
		☐	☐	☐	☐
(D) TOTAL	$				

DEBT REPAYMENT

Record any payments in excess of the minimum payment due.

CREDITOR	PAYMENT	BALANCE
(E) TOTAL	$	

WEEK THREE SUMMARY

CATEGORY	AMOUNT
(A) Income Total	
(B) Bills & Expenses Total	-
(C) Cash Envelopes Total	-
(D) Savings/Sinking Funds Total	-
(E) Debt Repayment Total	-
NOTE: Subtract B/C/D/E from A to determine what's left. **What's Left**	=

WEEKLY SPENDING LOG

Use the Weekly Spending Log to determine what your current spending habits are. Review the log to assess and correct impulse spending.

DATE	TRANSACTION	AMOUNT	Planned/Budgeted	Impulse Purchase
			○	○
			○	○
			○	○
			○	○
			○	○
			○	○
			○	○
			○	○
			○	○
			○	○
			○	○
			○	○
			○	○
			○	○
			○	○
			○	○
			○	○
			○	○
			○	○
			○	○
			○	○
			○	○
			○	○
			○	○
			○	○
			○	○
			○	○
			○	○
			○	○
			○	○
	TOTAL	$		

Spending *Plan*

Week of:

INCOME		Salary/Wages	Investment	Business	Side-Hustle
INCOME SOURCE	AMOUNT				
Rollover from previous week		☐	☐	☐	☐
		☐	☐	☐	☐
		☐	☐	☐	☐
		☐	☐	☐	☐
		☐	☐	☐	☐
		☐	☐	☐	☐
		☐	☐	☐	☐
(A) TOTAL	$				

BILLS & EXPENSES		Cash	Credit Card	Debit	Check
PAY TO	AMOUNT				
		☐	☐	☐	☐
		☐	☐	☐	☐
		☐	☐	☐	☐
		☐	☐	☐	☐
		☐	☐	☐	☐
		☐	☐	☐	☐
		☐	☐	☐	☐
		☐	☐	☐	☐
		☐	☐	☐	☐
		☐	☐	☐	☐
		☐	☐	☐	☐
		☐	☐	☐	☐
		☐	☐	☐	☐
		☐	☐	☐	☐
		☐	☐	☐	☐
(B) TOTAL	$				

Financial Priorities

This week's financial goal(s)

CASH ENVELOPES							
CATEGORY	AMOUNT	BANKING WITHDRAWAL DENOMINATIONS					
		$1	$5	$10	$20	$50	$100
		DENOMINATION TOTAL					
(C) TOTAL	$						

SAVINGS/SINKING FUNDS

ACCOUNT	AMOUNT	Sinking Fund	Short Term	Long Term	Retirement
		☐	☐	☐	☐
		☐	☐	☐	☐
		☐	☐	☐	☐
		☐	☐	☐	☐
		☐	☐	☐	☐
		☐	☐	☐	☐
		☐	☐	☐	☐
		☐	☐	☐	☐
		☐	☐	☐	☐
		☐	☐	☐	☐
(D) TOTAL	$				

DEBT REPAYMENT

Record any payments in excess of the minimum payment due.

CREDITOR	PAYMENT	BALANCE
(E) TOTAL	$	

WEEK FOUR SUMMARY

CATEGORY	AMOUNT
(A) Income Total	
(B) Bills & Expenses Total	-
(C) Cash Envelopes Total	-
(D) Savings/Sinking Funds Total	-
(E) Debt Repayment Total	-
NOTE: Subtract B/C/D/E from A to determine what's left. **What's Left**	=

WEEKLY SPENDING LOG

Use the Weekly Spending Log to determine what your current spending habits are. Review the log to assess and correct impulse spending.

DATE	TRANSACTION	AMOUNT	Planned/Budgeted	Impulse Purchase
			○	○
			○	○
			○	○
			○	○
			○	○
			○	○
			○	○
			○	○
			○	○
			○	○
			○	○
			○	○
			○	○
			○	○
			○	○
			○	○
			○	○
			○	○
			○	○
			○	○
			○	○
			○	○
			○	○
			○	○
			○	○
			○	○
			○	○
			○	○
			○	○
			○	○
			○	○
	TOTAL	$		

Spending *Plan*

Week of:

INCOME		Salary/Wages	Investment	Business	Side-Hustle
INCOME SOURCE	AMOUNT				
Rollover from previous week		☐	☐	☐	☐
		☐	☐	☐	☐
		☐	☐	☐	☐
		☐	☐	☐	☐
		☐	☐	☐	☐
		☐	☐	☐	☐
		☐	☐	☐	☐
(A) TOTAL	$				

BILLS & EXPENSES		Cash	Credit Card	Debit	Check
PAY TO	AMOUNT				
		☐	☐	☐	☐
		☐	☐	☐	☐
		☐	☐	☐	☐
		☐	☐	☐	☐
		☐	☐	☐	☐
		☐	☐	☐	☐
		☐	☐	☐	☐
		☐	☐	☐	☐
		☐	☐	☐	☐
		☐	☐	☐	☐
		☐	☐	☐	☐
		☐	☐	☐	☐
		☐	☐	☐	☐
		☐	☐	☐	☐
		☐	☐	☐	☐
(B) TOTAL	$				

Financial Priorities

This week's financial goal(s)

CASH ENVELOPES							
CATEGORY	AMOUNT	BANKING WITHDRAWAL DENOMINATIONS					
		$1	$5	$10	$20	$50	$100
		DENOMINATION TOTAL					
(C) TOTAL	$						

SAVINGS/SINKING FUNDS

ACCOUNT	AMOUNT	Sinking Fund	Short Term	Long Term	Retirement
		☐	☐	☐	☐
		☐	☐	☐	☐
		☐	☐	☐	☐
		☐	☐	☐	☐
		☐	☐	☐	☐
		☐	☐	☐	☐
		☐	☐	☐	☐
		☐	☐	☐	☐
		☐	☐	☐	☐
		☐	☐	☐	☐
(D) TOTAL	$				

DEBT REPAYMENT

Record any payments in excess of the minimum payment due.

CREDITOR	PAYMENT	BALANCE
(E) TOTAL	$	

WEEK FIVE SUMMARY

CATEGORY	AMOUNT
(A) Income Total	
(B) Bills & Expenses Total	-
(C) Cash Envelopes Total	-
(D) Savings/Sinking Funds Total	-
(E) Debt Repayment Total	-
NOTE: Subtract B/C/D/E from A to determine what's left. **What's Left**	=

WEEKLY SPENDING LOG

Use the Weekly Spending Log to determine what your current spending habits are. Review the log to assess and correct impulse spending.

DATE	TRANSACTION	AMOUNT	Planned/Budgeted	Impulse Purchase
			○	○
			○	○
			○	○
			○	○
			○	○
			○	○
			○	○
			○	○
			○	○
			○	○
			○	○
			○	○
			○	○
			○	○
			○	○
			○	○
			○	○
			○	○
			○	○
			○	○
			○	○
			○	○
			○	○
			○	○
			○	○
			○	○
			○	○
			○	○
			○	○
			○	○
	TOTAL	$		

Monthly Spending *summary*

Income	
Week One	
Week Two	
Week Three	
Week Four	
Week Five	
(A) TOTAL	$

Bills and Expenses	
Week One	
Week Two	
Week Three	
Week Four	
Week Five	
(B) TOTAL	$

Cash Envelopes	
Week One	
Week Two	
Week Three	
Week Four	
Week Five	
(C) TOTAL	$

Savings/Sinking Funds	
Week One	
Week Two	
Week Three	
Week Four	
Week Five	
(D) TOTAL	$

Debt Repayment	
Week One	
Week Two	
Week Three	
Week Four	
Week Five	
(E) TOTAL	$

MONTHLY SUMMARY	
(A) Income Total	
(B) Bills & Expenses Total	-
(C) Cash Envelopes Total	-
(D) Savings/SF Total	-
(E) Debt Repayment Total	-
What's Left	=

Subtract B/C/D/E from A to determine what's left.

Spending Assessment

Are there expenditures in your spending plan that can be cut or reduced? If yes, list the details below.

Impulse Spending

Review the spending log for each week, then calculate the total amount of the transactions listed as impulse purchases.

$

notes/observations

30-Day No Spend *challenge*

JAN FEB MAR APR MAY JUN JUL AUG SEP OCT NOV DEC

Place a check mark on the purse which corresponds to each day that you do not make an impulse or non-essential purchase.

Total number of no-spend days

1	2	3	4	5
6	7	8	9	10
11	12	13	14	15
16	17	18	19	20
21	22	23	24	25
26	27	28	29	30

notes

Stay *focused*

"It's not how much money you make, but how much money you keep, how hard it works for you, and how many generations you keep it for."

MONTH SIX

Bill and Income *calendar*

FINANCIAL GOALS

MONDAY	TUESDAY	WEDNESDAY

FINANCIAL GOALS

JAN FEB MAR APR MAY JUN JUL AUG SEP OCT NOV DEC

THURSDAY	FRIDAY	SATURDAY	SUNDAY

Spending *Plan*

Week of:

INCOME					
INCOME SOURCE	AMOUNT	Salary/Wages	Investment	Business	Side-Hustle
Rollover from previous week		☐	☐	☐	☐
		☐	☐	☐	☐
		☐	☐	☐	☐
		☐	☐	☐	☐
		☐	☐	☐	☐
		☐	☐	☐	☐
		☐	☐	☐	☐
(A) TOTAL	$				

BILLS & EXPENSES					
PAY TO	AMOUNT	Cash	Credit Card	Debit	Check
		☐	☐	☐	☐
		☐	☐	☐	☐
		☐	☐	☐	☐
		☐	☐	☐	☐
		☐	☐	☐	☐
		☐	☐	☐	☐
		☐	☐	☐	☐
		☐	☐	☐	☐
		☐	☐	☐	☐
		☐	☐	☐	☐
		☐	☐	☐	☐
		☐	☐	☐	☐
		☐	☐	☐	☐
		☐	☐	☐	☐
		☐	☐	☐	☐
(B) TOTAL	$				

Financial Priorities

This week's financial goal(s)

CASH ENVELOPES							
CATEGORY	AMOUNT	BANKING WITHDRAWAL DENOMINATIONS					
		$1	$5	$10	$20	$50	$100
		DENOMINATION TOTAL					
(C) TOTAL	$						

SAVINGS/SINKING FUNDS

ACCOUNT	AMOUNT	Sinking Fund	Short Term	Long Term	Retirement
		☐	☐	☐	☐
		☐	☐	☐	☐
		☐	☐	☐	☐
		☐	☐	☐	☐
		☐	☐	☐	☐
		☐	☐	☐	☐
		☐	☐	☐	☐
		☐	☐	☐	☐
		☐	☐	☐	☐
		☐	☐	☐	☐
(D) TOTAL	$				

DEBT REPAYMENT

Record any payments in excess of the minimum payment due.

CREDITOR	PAYMENT	BALANCE
(E) TOTAL	$	

WEEK ONE SUMMARY

CATEGORY	AMOUNT
(A) Income Total	
(B) Bills & Expenses Total	-
(C) Cash Envelopes Total	-
(D) Savings/Sinking Funds Total	-
(E) Debt Repayment Total	-
NOTE: Subtract B/C/D/E from A to determine what's left. **What's Left**	=

WEEKLY SPENDING LOG

Use the Weekly Spending Log to determine what your current spending habits are. Review the log to assess and correct impulse spending.

DATE	TRANSACTION	AMOUNT	Planned/Budgeted	Impulse Purchase
			○	○
			○	○
			○	○
			○	○
			○	○
			○	○
			○	○
			○	○
			○	○
			○	○
			○	○
			○	○
			○	○
			○	○
			○	○
			○	○
			○	○
			○	○
			○	○
			○	○
			○	○
			○	○
			○	○
			○	○
			○	○
			○	○
			○	○
			○	○
			○	○
			○	○
	TOTAL	$		

Spending *Plan*

Week of:

INCOME		Salary/Wages	Investment	Business	Side-Hustle
INCOME SOURCE	AMOUNT				
Rollover from previous week		☐	☐	☐	☐
		☐	☐	☐	☐
		☐	☐	☐	☐
		☐	☐	☐	☐
		☐	☐	☐	☐
		☐	☐	☐	☐
		☐	☐	☐	☐
(A) TOTAL	$				

BILLS & EXPENSES		Cash	Credit Card	Debit	Check
PAY TO	AMOUNT				
		☐	☐	☐	☐
		☐	☐	☐	☐
		☐	☐	☐	☐
		☐	☐	☐	☐
		☐	☐	☐	☐
		☐	☐	☐	☐
		☐	☐	☐	☐
		☐	☐	☐	☐
		☐	☐	☐	☐
		☐	☐	☐	☐
		☐	☐	☐	☐
		☐	☐	☐	☐
		☐	☐	☐	☐
		☐	☐	☐	☐
		☐	☐	☐	☐
(B) TOTAL	$				

Financial Priorities

This week's financial goal(s)

CASH ENVELOPES							
CATEGORY	AMOUNT	BANKING WITHDRAWAL DENOMINATIONS					
		$1	$5	$10	$20	$50	$100
		DENOMINATION TOTAL					
(C) TOTAL	$						

SAVINGS/SINKING FUNDS

ACCOUNT	AMOUNT	Sinking Fund	Short Term	Long Term	Retirement
		☐	☐	☐	☐
		☐	☐	☐	☐
		☐	☐	☐	☐
		☐	☐	☐	☐
		☐	☐	☐	☐
		☐	☐	☐	☐
		☐	☐	☐	☐
		☐	☐	☐	☐
		☐	☐	☐	☐
		☐	☐	☐	☐
(D) TOTAL	$				

DEBT REPAYMENT

Record any payments in excess of the minimum payment due.

CREDITOR	PAYMENT	BALANCE
(E) TOTAL	$	

WEEK TWO SUMMARY

CATEGORY	AMOUNT
(A) Income Total	
(B) Bills & Expenses Total	-
(C) Cash Envelopes Total	-
(D) Savings/Sinking Funds Total	-
(E) Debt Repayment Total	-
NOTE: Subtract B/C/D/E from A to determine what's left. **What's Left**	=

WEEKLY SPENDING LOG

Use the Weekly Spending Log to determine what your current spending habits are. Review the log to assess and correct impulse spending.

DATE	TRANSACTION	AMOUNT	Planned/Budgeted	Impulse Purchase
			○	○
			○	○
			○	○
			○	○
			○	○
			○	○
			○	○
			○	○
			○	○
			○	○
			○	○
			○	○
			○	○
			○	○
			○	○
			○	○
			○	○
			○	○
			○	○
			○	○
			○	○
			○	○
			○	○
			○	○
			○	○
			○	○
			○	○
			○	○
			○	○
			○	○
	TOTAL	$		

Spending *Plan*

Week of:

Financial Priorities

This week's financial goal(s)

INCOME

INCOME SOURCE	AMOUNT	Salary/Wages	Investment	Business	Side-Hustle
Rollover from previous week		☐	☐	☐	☐
		☐	☐	☐	☐
		☐	☐	☐	☐
		☐	☐	☐	☐
		☐	☐	☐	☐
		☐	☐	☐	☐
		☐	☐	☐	☐
(A) TOTAL	$				

BILLS & EXPENSES

PAY TO	AMOUNT	Cash	Credit Card	Debit	Check
		☐	☐	☐	☐
		☐	☐	☐	☐
		☐	☐	☐	☐
		☐	☐	☐	☐
		☐	☐	☐	☐
		☐	☐	☐	☐
		☐	☐	☐	☐
		☐	☐	☐	☐
		☐	☐	☐	☐
		☐	☐	☐	☐
		☐	☐	☐	☐
		☐	☐	☐	☐
		☐	☐	☐	☐
		☐	☐	☐	☐
		☐	☐	☐	☐
(B) TOTAL	$				

CASH ENVELOPES

CATEGORY	AMOUNT	BANKING WITHDRAWAL DENOMINATIONS					
		$1	$5	$10	$20	$50	$100
		DENOMINATION TOTAL					
(C) TOTAL	$						

SAVINGS/SINKING FUNDS

ACCOUNT	AMOUNT	Sinking Fund	Short Term	Long Term	Retirement
		☐	☐	☐	☐
		☐	☐	☐	☐
		☐	☐	☐	☐
		☐	☐	☐	☐
		☐	☐	☐	☐
		☐	☐	☐	☐
		☐	☐	☐	☐
		☐	☐	☐	☐
		☐	☐	☐	☐
		☐	☐	☐	☐
(D) TOTAL	$				

DEBT REPAYMENT

Record any payments in excess of the minimum payment due.

CREDITOR	PAYMENT	BALANCE
(E) TOTAL	$	

WEEK THREE SUMMARY

CATEGORY	AMOUNT
(A) Income Total	
(B) Bills & Expenses Total	-
(C) Cash Envelopes Total	-
(D) Savings/Sinking Funds Total	-
(E) Debt Repayment Total	-
NOTE: Subtract B/C/D/E from A to determine what's left. **What's Left**	=

WEEKLY SPENDING LOG

Use the Weekly Spending Log to determine what your current spending habits are. Review the log to assess and correct impulse spending.

DATE	TRANSACTION	AMOUNT	Planned/Budgeted	Impulse Purchase
			○	○
			○	○
			○	○
			○	○
			○	○
			○	○
			○	○
			○	○
			○	○
			○	○
			○	○
			○	○
			○	○
			○	○
			○	○
			○	○
			○	○
			○	○
			○	○
			○	○
			○	○
			○	○
			○	○
			○	○
			○	○
			○	○
			○	○
			○	○
			○	○
			○	○
	TOTAL	$		

Spending *Plan*

Week of:

INCOME		Salary/Wages	Investment	Business	Side-Hustle
INCOME SOURCE	AMOUNT				
Rollover from previous week		☐	☐	☐	☐
		☐	☐	☐	☐
		☐	☐	☐	☐
		☐	☐	☐	☐
		☐	☐	☐	☐
		☐	☐	☐	☐
		☐	☐	☐	☐
(A) TOTAL	$				

BILLS & EXPENSES		Cash	Credit Card	Debit	Check
PAY TO	AMOUNT				
		☐	☐	☐	☐
		☐	☐	☐	☐
		☐	☐	☐	☐
		☐	☐	☐	☐
		☐	☐	☐	☐
		☐	☐	☐	☐
		☐	☐	☐	☐
		☐	☐	☐	☐
		☐	☐	☐	☐
		☐	☐	☐	☐
		☐	☐	☐	☐
		☐	☐	☐	☐
		☐	☐	☐	☐
		☐	☐	☐	☐
		☐	☐	☐	☐
(B) TOTAL	$				

Financial Priorities

This week's financial goal(s)

CASH ENVELOPES							
CATEGORY	AMOUNT	BANKING WITHDRAWAL DENOMINATIONS					
		$1	$5	$10	$20	$50	$100
		DENOMINATION TOTAL					
(C) TOTAL	$						

SAVINGS/SINKING FUNDS

ACCOUNT	AMOUNT	Sinking Fund	Short Term	Long Term	Retirement
		☐	☐	☐	☐
		☐	☐	☐	☐
		☐	☐	☐	☐
		☐	☐	☐	☐
		☐	☐	☐	☐
		☐	☐	☐	☐
		☐	☐	☐	☐
		☐	☐	☐	☐
		☐	☐	☐	☐
		☐	☐	☐	☐
(D) TOTAL	$				

DEBT REPAYMENT

Record any payments in excess of the minimum payment due.

CREDITOR	PAYMENT	BALANCE
(E) TOTAL	$	

WEEK FOUR SUMMARY

CATEGORY	AMOUNT
(A) Income Total	
(B) Bills & Expenses Total	-
(C) Cash Envelopes Total	-
(D) Savings/Sinking Funds Total	-
(E) Debt Repayment Total	-
NOTE: Subtract B/C/D/E from A to determine what's left. **What's Left**	=

WEEKLY SPENDING LOG

Use the Weekly Spending Log to determine what your current spending habits are. Review the log to assess and correct impulse spending.

DATE	TRANSACTION	AMOUNT	Planned/Budgeted	Impulse Purchase
			○	○
			○	○
			○	○
			○	○
			○	○
			○	○
			○	○
			○	○
			○	○
			○	○
			○	○
			○	○
			○	○
			○	○
			○	○
			○	○
			○	○
			○	○
			○	○
			○	○
			○	○
			○	○
			○	○
			○	○
			○	○
			○	○
			○	○
			○	○
			○	○
			○	○
			○	○
	TOTAL	$		

Spending *Plan*

Week of:

INCOME					
INCOME SOURCE	AMOUNT	Salary/Wages	Investment	Business	Side-Hustle
Rollover from previous week		☐	☐	☐	☐
		☐	☐	☐	☐
		☐	☐	☐	☐
		☐	☐	☐	☐
		☐	☐	☐	☐
		☐	☐	☐	☐
		☐	☐	☐	☐
(A) TOTAL	$				

BILLS & EXPENSES					
PAY TO	AMOUNT	Cash	Credit Card	Debit	Check
		☐	☐	☐	☐
		☐	☐	☐	☐
		☐	☐	☐	☐
		☐	☐	☐	☐
		☐	☐	☐	☐
		☐	☐	☐	☐
		☐	☐	☐	☐
		☐	☐	☐	☐
		☐	☐	☐	☐
		☐	☐	☐	☐
		☐	☐	☐	☐
		☐	☐	☐	☐
		☐	☐	☐	☐
		☐	☐	☐	☐
		☐	☐	☐	☐
(B) TOTAL	$				

Financial Priorities

This week's financial goal(s)

CASH ENVELOPES							
CATEGORY	AMOUNT	BANKING WITHDRAWAL DENOMINATIONS					
		$1	$5	$10	$20	$50	$100
		DENOMINATION TOTAL					
(C) TOTAL	$						

SAVINGS/SINKING FUNDS

ACCOUNT	AMOUNT	Sinking Fund	Short Term	Long Term	Retirement
		☐	☐	☐	☐
		☐	☐	☐	☐
		☐	☐	☐	☐
		☐	☐	☐	☐
		☐	☐	☐	☐
		☐	☐	☐	☐
		☐	☐	☐	☐
		☐	☐	☐	☐
		☐	☐	☐	☐
		☐	☐	☐	☐
(D) TOTAL	$				

DEBT REPAYMENT

Record any payments in excess of the minimum payment due.

CREDITOR	PAYMENT	BALANCE
(E) TOTAL	$	

WEEK FIVE SUMMARY

CATEGORY	AMOUNT
(A) Income Total	
(B) Bills & Expenses Total	-
(C) Cash Envelopes Total	-
(D) Savings/Sinking Funds Total	-
(E) Debt Repayment Total	-
NOTE: Subtract B/C/D/E from A to determine what's left. **What's Left**	=

WEEKLY SPENDING LOG

Use the Weekly Spending Log to determine what your current spending habits are. Review the log to assess and correct impulse spending.

DATE	TRANSACTION	AMOUNT	Planned/Budgeted	Impulse Purchase
			○	○
			○	○
			○	○
			○	○
			○	○
			○	○
			○	○
			○	○
			○	○
			○	○
			○	○
			○	○
			○	○
			○	○
			○	○
			○	○
			○	○
			○	○
			○	○
			○	○
			○	○
			○	○
			○	○
			○	○
			○	○
			○	○
			○	○
			○	○
			○	○
			○	○
	TOTAL	$		

Monthly Spending *summary*

Income	
Week One	
Week Two	
Week Three	
Week Four	
Week Five	
(A) TOTAL	$

Bills and Expenses	
Week One	
Week Two	
Week Three	
Week Four	
Week Five	
(B) TOTAL	$

Spending Assessment

Are there expenditures in your spending plan that can be cut or reduced? If yes, list the details below.

Cash Envelopes	
Week One	
Week Two	
Week Three	
Week Four	
Week Five	
(C) TOTAL	$

Savings/Sinking Funds	
Week One	
Week Two	
Week Three	
Week Four	
Week Five	
(D) TOTAL	$

Impulse Spending

Review the spending log for each week, then calculate the total amount of the transactions listed as impulse purchases.

$

Debt Repayment	
Week One	
Week Two	
Week Three	
Week Four	
Week Five	
(E) TOTAL	$

MONTHLY SUMMARY	
(A) Income Total	
(B) Bills & Expenses Total	-
(C) Cash Envelopes Total	-
(D) Savings/SF Total	-
(E) Debt Repayment Total	-
What's Left	=

Subtract B/C/D/E from A to determine what's left.

notes/observations

30-Day No Spend *challenge*

JAN	FEB	MAR	APR	MAY	JUN	JUL	AUG	SEP	OCT	NOV	DEC

Place a check mark on the purse which corresponds to each day that you do not make an impulse or non-essential purchase.

Total number of no-spend days

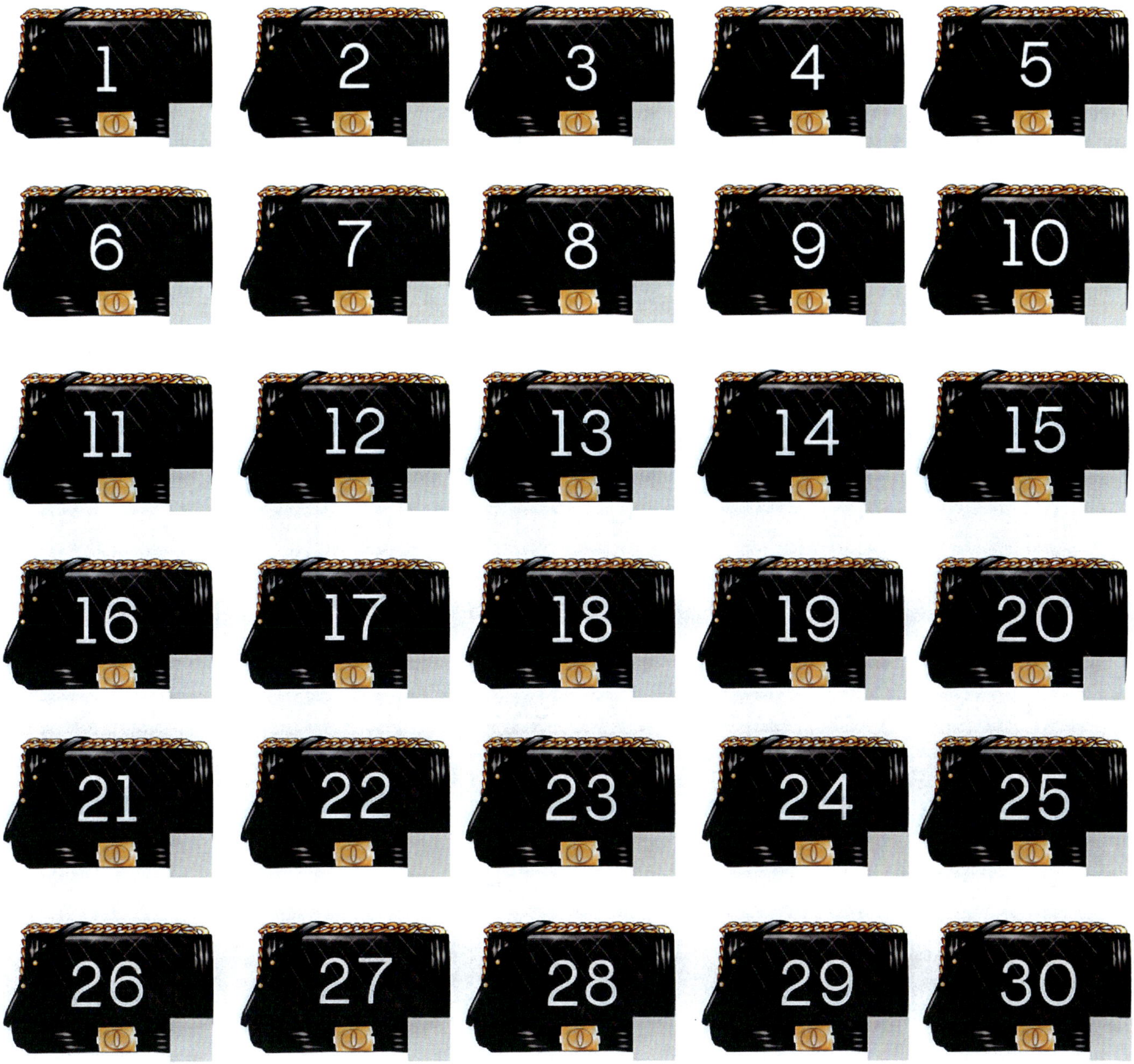

notes

Stay *focused*

"It's not how much money you make, but how much money you keep, how hard it works for you, and how many generations you keep it for."

MONTH SEVEN

Bill and Income *calendar*

FINANCIAL GOALS

MONDAY	TUESDAY	WEDNESDAY

JAN FEB MAR APR MAY JUN JUL AUG SEP OCT NOV DEC

THURSDAY	FRIDAY	SATURDAY	SUNDAY

Spending *Plan*

Week of:

INCOME		Salary/Wages	Investment	Business	Side-Hustle
INCOME SOURCE	AMOUNT				
Rollover from previous week		☐	☐	☐	☐
		☐	☐	☐	☐
		☐	☐	☐	☐
		☐	☐	☐	☐
		☐	☐	☐	☐
		☐	☐	☐	☐
		☐	☐	☐	☐
(A) TOTAL	$				

BILLS & EXPENSES		Cash	Credit Card	Debit	Check
PAY TO	AMOUNT				
		☐	☐	☐	☐
		☐	☐	☐	☐
		☐	☐	☐	☐
		☐	☐	☐	☐
		☐	☐	☐	☐
		☐	☐	☐	☐
		☐	☐	☐	☐
		☐	☐	☐	☐
		☐	☐	☐	☐
		☐	☐	☐	☐
		☐	☐	☐	☐
		☐	☐	☐	☐
		☐	☐	☐	☐
		☐	☐	☐	☐
		☐	☐	☐	☐
(B) TOTAL	$				

Financial Priorities

This week's financial goal(s)

CASH ENVELOPES							
CATEGORY	AMOUNT	BANKING WITHDRAWAL DENOMINATIONS					
		$1	$5	$10	$20	$50	$100
		DENOMINATION TOTAL					
(C) TOTAL	$						

SAVINGS/SINKING FUNDS

ACCOUNT	AMOUNT	Sinking Fund	Short Term	Long Term	Retirement
		☐	☐	☐	☐
		☐	☐	☐	☐
		☐	☐	☐	☐
		☐	☐	☐	☐
		☐	☐	☐	☐
		☐	☐	☐	☐
		☐	☐	☐	☐
		☐	☐	☐	☐
		☐	☐	☐	☐
		☐	☐	☐	☐
(D) TOTAL	$				

DEBT REPAYMENT

Record any payments in excess of the minimum payment due.

CREDITOR	PAYMENT	BALANCE
(E) TOTAL	$	

WEEK ONE SUMMARY

CATEGORY	AMOUNT
(A) Income Total	
(B) Bills & Expenses Total	-
(C) Cash Envelopes Total	-
(D) Savings/Sinking Funds Total	-
(E) Debt Repayment Total	-
NOTE: Subtract B/C/D/E from A to determine what's left. **What's Left**	=

WEEKLY SPENDING LOG

Use the Weekly Spending Log to determine what your current spending habits are. Review the log to assess and correct impulse spending.

DATE	TRANSACTION	AMOUNT	Planned/Budgeted	Impulse Purchase
			○	○
			○	○
			○	○
			○	○
			○	○
			○	○
			○	○
			○	○
			○	○
			○	○
			○	○
			○	○
			○	○
			○	○
			○	○
			○	○
			○	○
			○	○
			○	○
			○	○
			○	○
			○	○
			○	○
			○	○
			○	○
			○	○
			○	○
			○	○
			○	○
			○	○
			○	○
			○	○
	TOTAL	$		

Spending *Plan*

Week of:

INCOME		Salary/Wages	Investment	Business	Side-Hustle
INCOME SOURCE	AMOUNT				
Rollover from previous week		☐	☐	☐	☐
		☐	☐	☐	☐
		☐	☐	☐	☐
		☐	☐	☐	☐
		☐	☐	☐	☐
		☐	☐	☐	☐
		☐	☐	☐	☐
(A) TOTAL	$				

BILLS & EXPENSES		Cash	Credit Card	Debit	Check
PAY TO	AMOUNT				
		☐	☐	☐	☐
		☐	☐	☐	☐
		☐	☐	☐	☐
		☐	☐	☐	☐
		☐	☐	☐	☐
		☐	☐	☐	☐
		☐	☐	☐	☐
		☐	☐	☐	☐
		☐	☐	☐	☐
		☐	☐	☐	☐
		☐	☐	☐	☐
		☐	☐	☐	☐
		☐	☐	☐	☐
		☐	☐	☐	☐
		☐	☐	☐	☐
(B) TOTAL	$				

Financial Priorities

This week's financial goal(s)

CASH ENVELOPES							
CATEGORY	AMOUNT	BANKING WITHDRAWAL DENOMINATIONS					
		$1	$5	$10	$20	$50	$100
		DENOMINATION TOTAL					
(C) TOTAL	$						

SAVINGS/SINKING FUNDS

ACCOUNT	AMOUNT	Sinking Fund	Short Term	Long Term	Retirement
		☐	☐	☐	☐
		☐	☐	☐	☐
		☐	☐	☐	☐
		☐	☐	☐	☐
		☐	☐	☐	☐
		☐	☐	☐	☐
		☐	☐	☐	☐
		☐	☐	☐	☐
		☐	☐	☐	☐
		☐	☐	☐	☐
(D) TOTAL	$				

DEBT REPAYMENT

Record any payments in excess of the minimum payment due.

CREDITOR	PAYMENT	BALANCE
(E) TOTAL	$	

WEEK TWO SUMMARY

CATEGORY	AMOUNT
(A) Income Total	
(B) Bills & Expenses Total	-
(C) Cash Envelopes Total	-
(D) Savings/Sinking Funds Total	-
(E) Debt Repayment Total	-
NOTE: Subtract B/C/D/E from A to determine what's left. **What's Left**	=

WEEKLY SPENDING LOG

Use the Weekly Spending Log to determine what your current spending habits are. Review the log to assess and correct impulse spending.

DATE	TRANSACTION	AMOUNT	Planned/Budgeted	Impulse Purchase
			○	○
			○	○
			○	○
			○	○
			○	○
			○	○
			○	○
			○	○
			○	○
			○	○
			○	○
			○	○
			○	○
			○	○
			○	○
			○	○
			○	○
			○	○
			○	○
			○	○
			○	○
			○	○
			○	○
			○	○
			○	○
			○	○
			○	○
			○	○
			○	○
			○	○
	TOTAL	$		

Spending *Plan*

Week of:

INCOME					
INCOME SOURCE	AMOUNT	Salary/Wages	Investment	Business	Side-Hustle
Rollover from previous week		☐	☐	☐	☐
		☐	☐	☐	☐
		☐	☐	☐	☐
		☐	☐	☐	☐
		☐	☐	☐	☐
		☐	☐	☐	☐
		☐	☐	☐	☐
(A) TOTAL	$				

BILLS & EXPENSES					
PAY TO	AMOUNT	Cash	Credit Card	Debit	Check
		☐	☐	☐	☐
		☐	☐	☐	☐
		☐	☐	☐	☐
		☐	☐	☐	☐
		☐	☐	☐	☐
		☐	☐	☐	☐
		☐	☐	☐	☐
		☐	☐	☐	☐
		☐	☐	☐	☐
		☐	☐	☐	☐
		☐	☐	☐	☐
		☐	☐	☐	☐
		☐	☐	☐	☐
		☐	☐	☐	☐
		☐	☐	☐	☐
(B) TOTAL	$				

Financial Priorities

This week's financial goal(s)

CASH ENVELOPES							
CATEGORY	AMOUNT	BANKING WITHDRAWAL DENOMINATIONS					
		$1	$5	$10	$20	$50	$100
		DENOMINATION TOTAL					
(C) TOTAL	$						

SAVINGS/SINKING FUNDS

ACCOUNT	AMOUNT	Sinking Fund	Short Term	Long Term	Retirement
		☐	☐	☐	☐
		☐	☐	☐	☐
		☐	☐	☐	☐
		☐	☐	☐	☐
		☐	☐	☐	☐
		☐	☐	☐	☐
		☐	☐	☐	☐
		☐	☐	☐	☐
		☐	☐	☐	☐
		☐	☐	☐	☐
(D) TOTAL	$				

DEBT REPAYMENT

Record any payments in excess of the minimum payment due.

CREDITOR	PAYMENT	BALANCE
(E) TOTAL	$	

WEEK THREE SUMMARY

CATEGORY	AMOUNT
(A) Income Total	
(B) Bills & Expenses Total	-
(C) Cash Envelopes Total	-
(D) Savings/Sinking Funds Total	-
(E) Debt Repayment Total	-
NOTE: Subtract B/C/D/E from A to determine what's left. **What's Left**	=

WEEKLY SPENDING LOG

Use the Weekly Spending Log to determine what your current spending habits are. Review the log to assess and correct impulse spending.

DATE	TRANSACTION	AMOUNT	Planned/Budgeted	Impulse Purchase
			○	○
			○	○
			○	○
			○	○
			○	○
			○	○
			○	○
			○	○
			○	○
			○	○
			○	○
			○	○
			○	○
			○	○
			○	○
			○	○
			○	○
			○	○
			○	○
			○	○
			○	○
			○	○
			○	○
			○	○
			○	○
			○	○
			○	○
			○	○
			○	○
			○	○
	TOTAL	$		

Spending *Plan*

Week of:

INCOME		Salary/Wages	Investment	Business	Side-Hustle
INCOME SOURCE	AMOUNT				
Rollover from previous week		☐	☐	☐	☐
		☐	☐	☐	☐
		☐	☐	☐	☐
		☐	☐	☐	☐
		☐	☐	☐	☐
		☐	☐	☐	☐
		☐	☐	☐	☐
(A) TOTAL	$				

BILLS & EXPENSES		Cash	Credit Card	Debit	Check
PAY TO	AMOUNT				
		☐	☐	☐	☐
		☐	☐	☐	☐
		☐	☐	☐	☐
		☐	☐	☐	☐
		☐	☐	☐	☐
		☐	☐	☐	☐
		☐	☐	☐	☐
		☐	☐	☐	☐
		☐	☐	☐	☐
		☐	☐	☐	☐
		☐	☐	☐	☐
		☐	☐	☐	☐
		☐	☐	☐	☐
		☐	☐	☐	☐
		☐	☐	☐	☐
(B) TOTAL	$				

Financial Priorities

This week's financial goal(s)

CASH ENVELOPES							
CATEGORY	AMOUNT	BANKING WITHDRAWAL DENOMINATIONS					
		$1	$5	$10	$20	$50	$100
		DENOMINATION TOTAL					
(C) TOTAL	$						

SAVINGS/SINKING FUNDS

ACCOUNT	AMOUNT	Sinking Fund	Short Term	Long Term	Retirement
		☐	☐	☐	☐
		☐	☐	☐	☐
		☐	☐	☐	☐
		☐	☐	☐	☐
		☐	☐	☐	☐
		☐	☐	☐	☐
		☐	☐	☐	☐
		☐	☐	☐	☐
		☐	☐	☐	☐
		☐	☐	☐	☐
(D) TOTAL	$				

DEBT REPAYMENT

Record any payments in excess of the minimum payment due.

CREDITOR	PAYMENT	BALANCE
(E) TOTAL	$	

WEEK FOUR SUMMARY

CATEGORY	AMOUNT
(A) Income Total	
(B) Bills & Expenses Total	-
(C) Cash Envelopes Total	-
(D) Savings/Sinking Funds Total	-
(E) Debt Repayment Total	-
NOTE: Subtract B/C/D/E from A to determine what's left. **What's Left**	=

WEEKLY SPENDING LOG

Use the Weekly Spending Log to determine what your current spending habits are. Review the log to assess and correct impulse spending.

DATE	TRANSACTION	AMOUNT	Planned/Budgeted	Impulse Purchase
			○	○
			○	○
			○	○
			○	○
			○	○
			○	○
			○	○
			○	○
			○	○
			○	○
			○	○
			○	○
			○	○
			○	○
			○	○
			○	○
			○	○
			○	○
			○	○
			○	○
			○	○
			○	○
			○	○
			○	○
			○	○
			○	○
			○	○
			○	○
			○	○
			○	○
	TOTAL	$		

Spending *Plan*

Week of:

INCOME		Salary/Wages	Investment	Business	Side-Hustle
INCOME SOURCE	AMOUNT				
Rollover from previous week		☐	☐	☐	☐
		☐	☐	☐	☐
		☐	☐	☐	☐
		☐	☐	☐	☐
		☐	☐	☐	☐
		☐	☐	☐	☐
		☐	☐	☐	☐
(A) TOTAL	$				

BILLS & EXPENSES		Cash	Credit Card	Debit	Check
PAY TO	AMOUNT				
		☐	☐	☐	☐
		☐	☐	☐	☐
		☐	☐	☐	☐
		☐	☐	☐	☐
		☐	☐	☐	☐
		☐	☐	☐	☐
		☐	☐	☐	☐
		☐	☐	☐	☐
		☐	☐	☐	☐
		☐	☐	☐	☐
		☐	☐	☐	☐
		☐	☐	☐	☐
		☐	☐	☐	☐
		☐	☐	☐	☐
		☐	☐	☐	☐
(B) TOTAL	$				

Financial Priorities

This week's financial goal(s)

CASH ENVELOPES							
CATEGORY	AMOUNT	BANKING WITHDRAWAL DENOMINATIONS					
		$1	$5	$10	$20	$50	$100
		DENOMINATION TOTAL					
(C) TOTAL	$						

SAVINGS/SINKING FUNDS

ACCOUNT	AMOUNT	Sinking Fund	Short Term	Long Term	Retirement
		☐	☐	☐	☐
		☐	☐	☐	☐
		☐	☐	☐	☐
		☐	☐	☐	☐
		☐	☐	☐	☐
		☐	☐	☐	☐
		☐	☐	☐	☐
		☐	☐	☐	☐
		☐	☐	☐	☐
		☐	☐	☐	☐
(D) TOTAL	$				

DEBT REPAYMENT

Record any payments in excess of the minimum payment due.

CREDITOR	PAYMENT	BALANCE
(E) TOTAL	$	

WEEK FIVE SUMMARY

CATEGORY	AMOUNT
(A) Income Total	
(B) Bills & Expenses Total	-
(C) Cash Envelopes Total	-
(D) Savings/Sinking Funds Total	-
(E) Debt Repayment Total	-
NOTE: Subtract B/C/D/E from A to determine what's left. **What's Left**	=

WEEKLY SPENDING LOG

Use the Weekly Spending Log to determine what your current spending habits are. Review the log to assess and correct impulse spending.

DATE	TRANSACTION	AMOUNT	Planned/Budgeted	Impulse Purchase
			○	○
			○	○
			○	○
			○	○
			○	○
			○	○
			○	○
			○	○
			○	○
			○	○
			○	○
			○	○
			○	○
			○	○
			○	○
			○	○
			○	○
			○	○
			○	○
			○	○
			○	○
			○	○
			○	○
			○	○
			○	○
			○	○
			○	○
			○	○
			○	○
			○	○
	TOTAL	$		

Monthly Spending *summary*

Income	
Week One	
Week Two	
Week Three	
Week Four	
Week Five	
(A) TOTAL	$

Bills and Expenses	
Week One	
Week Two	
Week Three	
Week Four	
Week Five	
(B) TOTAL	$

Cash Envelopes	
Week One	
Week Two	
Week Three	
Week Four	
Week Five	
(C) TOTAL	$

Savings/Sinking Funds	
Week One	
Week Two	
Week Three	
Week Four	
Week Five	
(D) TOTAL	$

Debt Repayment	
Week One	
Week Two	
Week Three	
Week Four	
Week Five	
(E) TOTAL	$

MONTHLY SUMMARY	
(A) Income Total	
(B) Bills & Expenses Total	-
(C) Cash Envelopes Total	-
(D) Savings/SF Total	-
(E) Debt Repayment Total	-
What's Left	=

Subtract B/C/D/E from A to determine what's left.

Spending Assessment

Are there expenditures in your spending plan that can be cut or reduced? If yes, list the details below.

Impulse Spending

Review the spending log for each week, then calculate the total amount of the transactions listed as impulse purchases.

$

notes/observations

30-Day No Spend *challenge*

JAN FEB MAR APR MAY JUN JUL AUG SEP OCT NOV DEC

Place a check mark on the purse which corresponds to each day that you do not make an impulse or non-essential purchase.

Total number of no-spend days

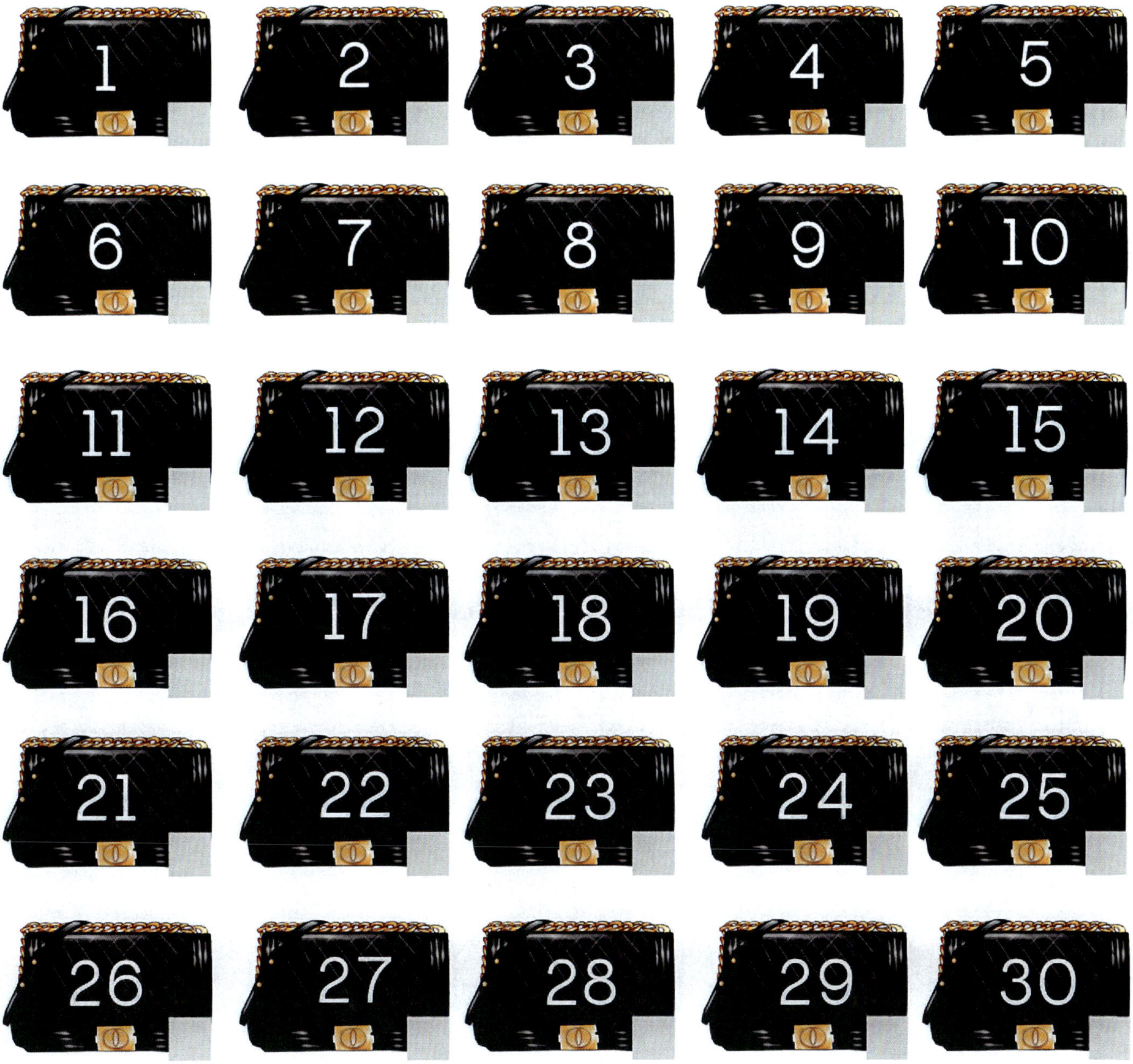

notes

Stay *focused*

"It's not how much money you make, but how much money you keep, how hard it works for you, and how many generations you keep it for."

MONTH EIGHT

Bill and Income *calendar*

FINANCIAL GOALS

MONDAY	TUESDAY	WEDNESDAY

JAN FEB MAR APR MAY JUN JUL AUG SEP OCT NOV DEC

THURSDAY	FRIDAY	SATURDAY	SUNDAY

Spending *Plan*

Week of:

INCOME		Salary/Wages	Investment	Business	Side-Hustle
INCOME SOURCE	AMOUNT				
Rollover from previous week		☐	☐	☐	☐
		☐	☐	☐	☐
		☐	☐	☐	☐
		☐	☐	☐	☐
		☐	☐	☐	☐
		☐	☐	☐	☐
		☐	☐	☐	☐
(A) TOTAL	$				

BILLS & EXPENSES		Cash	Credit Card	Debit	Check
PAY TO	AMOUNT				
		☐	☐	☐	☐
		☐	☐	☐	☐
		☐	☐	☐	☐
		☐	☐	☐	☐
		☐	☐	☐	☐
		☐	☐	☐	☐
		☐	☐	☐	☐
		☐	☐	☐	☐
		☐	☐	☐	☐
		☐	☐	☐	☐
		☐	☐	☐	☐
		☐	☐	☐	☐
		☐	☐	☐	☐
		☐	☐	☐	☐
		☐	☐	☐	☐
(B) TOTAL	$				

Financial Priorities

This week's financial goal(s)

CASH ENVELOPES							
CATEGORY	AMOUNT	BANKING WITHDRAWAL DENOMINATIONS					
		$1	$5	$10	$20	$50	$100
		DENOMINATION TOTAL					
(C) TOTAL	$						

SAVINGS/SINKING FUNDS

ACCOUNT	AMOUNT	Sinking Fund	Short Term	Long Term	Retirement
		☐	☐	☐	☐
		☐	☐	☐	☐
		☐	☐	☐	☐
		☐	☐	☐	☐
		☐	☐	☐	☐
		☐	☐	☐	☐
		☐	☐	☐	☐
		☐	☐	☐	☐
		☐	☐	☐	☐
		☐	☐	☐	☐
(D) TOTAL	$				

DEBT REPAYMENT

Record any payments in excess of the minimum payment due.

CREDITOR	PAYMENT	BALANCE
(E) TOTAL	$	

WEEK ONE SUMMARY

CATEGORY	AMOUNT
(A) Income Total	
(B) Bills & Expenses Total	-
(C) Cash Envelopes Total	-
(D) Savings/Sinking Funds Total	-
(E) Debt Repayment Total	-
NOTE: Subtract B/C/D/E from A to determine what's left. **What's Left**	=

WEEKLY SPENDING LOG

Use the Weekly Spending Log to determine what your current spending habits are. Review the log to assess and correct impulse spending.

DATE	TRANSACTION	AMOUNT	Planned/Budgeted	Impulse Purchase
			○	○
			○	○
			○	○
			○	○
			○	○
			○	○
			○	○
			○	○
			○	○
			○	○
			○	○
			○	○
			○	○
			○	○
			○	○
			○	○
			○	○
			○	○
			○	○
			○	○
			○	○
			○	○
			○	○
			○	○
			○	○
			○	○
			○	○
			○	○
			○	○
			○	○
	TOTAL	$		

Spending *Plan*

Week of:

INCOME		Salary/Wages	Investment	Business	Side-Hustle
INCOME SOURCE	AMOUNT				
Rollover from previous week		☐	☐	☐	☐
		☐	☐	☐	☐
		☐	☐	☐	☐
		☐	☐	☐	☐
		☐	☐	☐	☐
		☐	☐	☐	☐
		☐	☐	☐	☐
(A) TOTAL	$				

BILLS & EXPENSES		Cash	Credit Card	Debit	Check
PAY TO	AMOUNT				
		☐	☐	☐	☐
		☐	☐	☐	☐
		☐	☐	☐	☐
		☐	☐	☐	☐
		☐	☐	☐	☐
		☐	☐	☐	☐
		☐	☐	☐	☐
		☐	☐	☐	☐
		☐	☐	☐	☐
		☐	☐	☐	☐
		☐	☐	☐	☐
		☐	☐	☐	☐
		☐	☐	☐	☐
		☐	☐	☐	☐
		☐	☐	☐	☐
(B) TOTAL	$				

Financial Priorities

This week's financial goal(s)

CASH ENVELOPES							
CATEGORY	AMOUNT	BANKING WITHDRAWAL DENOMINATIONS					
		$1	$5	$10	$20	$50	$100
		DENOMINATION TOTAL					
(C) TOTAL	$						

SAVINGS/SINKING FUNDS

ACCOUNT	AMOUNT	Sinking Fund	Short Term	Long Term	Retirement
		☐	☐	☐	☐
		☐	☐	☐	☐
		☐	☐	☐	☐
		☐	☐	☐	☐
		☐	☐	☐	☐
		☐	☐	☐	☐
		☐	☐	☐	☐
		☐	☐	☐	☐
		☐	☐	☐	☐
		☐	☐	☐	☐
(D) TOTAL	$				

DEBT REPAYMENT

Record any payments in excess of the minimum payment due.

CREDITOR	PAYMENT	BALANCE
(E) TOTAL	$	

WEEK TWO SUMMARY

CATEGORY	AMOUNT
(A) Income Total	
(B) Bills & Expenses Total	-
(C) Cash Envelopes Total	-
(D) Savings/Sinking Funds Total	-
(E) Debt Repayment Total	-
NOTE: Subtract B/C/D/E from A to determine what's left. **What's Left**	=

WEEKLY SPENDING LOG

Use the Weekly Spending Log to determine what your current spending habits are. Review the log to assess and correct impulse spending.

DATE	TRANSACTION	AMOUNT	Planned/Budgeted	Impulse Purchase
			○	○
			○	○
			○	○
			○	○
			○	○
			○	○
			○	○
			○	○
			○	○
			○	○
			○	○
			○	○
			○	○
			○	○
			○	○
			○	○
			○	○
			○	○
			○	○
			○	○
			○	○
			○	○
			○	○
			○	○
			○	○
			○	○
			○	○
			○	○
			○	○
			○	○
	TOTAL	$		

Spending *Plan*

Week of:

Financial Priorities

This week's financial goal(s)

INCOME					
INCOME SOURCE	AMOUNT	Salary/Wages	Investment	Business	Side-Hustle
Rollover from previous week		☐	☐	☐	☐
		☐	☐	☐	☐
		☐	☐	☐	☐
		☐	☐	☐	☐
		☐	☐	☐	☐
		☐	☐	☐	☐
		☐	☐	☐	☐
(A) TOTAL	$				

BILLS & EXPENSES					
PAY TO	AMOUNT	Cash	Credit Card	Debit	Check
		☐	☐	☐	☐
		☐	☐	☐	☐
		☐	☐	☐	☐
		☐	☐	☐	☐
		☐	☐	☐	☐
		☐	☐	☐	☐
		☐	☐	☐	☐
		☐	☐	☐	☐
		☐	☐	☐	☐
		☐	☐	☐	☐
		☐	☐	☐	☐
		☐	☐	☐	☐
		☐	☐	☐	☐
		☐	☐	☐	☐
		☐	☐	☐	☐
(B) TOTAL	$				

CASH ENVELOPES							
CATEGORY	AMOUNT	BANKING WITHDRAWAL DENOMINATIONS					
		$1	$5	$10	$20	$50	$100
		DENOMINATION TOTAL					
(C) TOTAL	$						

SAVINGS/SINKING FUNDS

ACCOUNT	AMOUNT	Sinking Fund	Short Term	Long Term	Retirement
		☐	☐	☐	☐
		☐	☐	☐	☐
		☐	☐	☐	☐
		☐	☐	☐	☐
		☐	☐	☐	☐
		☐	☐	☐	☐
		☐	☐	☐	☐
		☐	☐	☐	☐
		☐	☐	☐	☐
		☐	☐	☐	☐
(D) TOTAL	$				

DEBT REPAYMENT

Record any payments in excess of the minimum payment due.

CREDITOR	PAYMENT	BALANCE
(E) TOTAL	$	

WEEK THREE SUMMARY

CATEGORY	AMOUNT
(A) Income Total	
(B) Bills & Expenses Total	-
(C) Cash Envelopes Total	-
(D) Savings/Sinking Funds Total	-
(E) Debt Repayment Total	-
NOTE: Subtract B/C/D/E from A to determine what's left. **What's Left**	=

WEEKLY SPENDING LOG

Use the Weekly Spending Log to determine what your current spending habits are. Review the log to assess and correct impulse spending.

DATE	TRANSACTION	AMOUNT	Planned/Budgeted	Impulse Purchase
			○	○
			○	○
			○	○
			○	○
			○	○
			○	○
			○	○
			○	○
			○	○
			○	○
			○	○
			○	○
			○	○
			○	○
			○	○
			○	○
			○	○
			○	○
			○	○
			○	○
			○	○
			○	○
			○	○
			○	○
			○	○
			○	○
			○	○
			○	○
			○	○
			○	○
	TOTAL	$		

Spending *Plan*

Week of:

INCOME		Salary/Wages	Investment	Business	Side-Hustle
INCOME SOURCE	AMOUNT				
Rollover from previous week		☐	☐	☐	☐
		☐	☐	☐	☐
		☐	☐	☐	☐
		☐	☐	☐	☐
		☐	☐	☐	☐
		☐	☐	☐	☐
		☐	☐	☐	☐
(A) TOTAL	$				

BILLS & EXPENSES		Cash	Credit Card	Debit	Check
PAY TO	AMOUNT				
		☐	☐	☐	☐
		☐	☐	☐	☐
		☐	☐	☐	☐
		☐	☐	☐	☐
		☐	☐	☐	☐
		☐	☐	☐	☐
		☐	☐	☐	☐
		☐	☐	☐	☐
		☐	☐	☐	☐
		☐	☐	☐	☐
		☐	☐	☐	☐
		☐	☐	☐	☐
		☐	☐	☐	☐
		☐	☐	☐	☐
		☐	☐	☐	☐
(B) TOTAL	$				

Financial Priorities

This week's financial goal(s)

CASH ENVELOPES							
CATEGORY	AMOUNT	BANKING WITHDRAWAL DENOMINATIONS					
		$1	$5	$10	$20	$50	$100
		DENOMINATION TOTAL					
(C) TOTAL	$						

SAVINGS/SINKING FUNDS

ACCOUNT	AMOUNT	Sinking Fund	Short Term	Long Term	Retirement
		☐	☐	☐	☐
		☐	☐	☐	☐
		☐	☐	☐	☐
		☐	☐	☐	☐
		☐	☐	☐	☐
		☐	☐	☐	☐
		☐	☐	☐	☐
		☐	☐	☐	☐
		☐	☐	☐	☐
		☐	☐	☐	☐
(D) TOTAL	$				

DEBT REPAYMENT

Record any payments in excess of the minimum payment due.

CREDITOR	PAYMENT	BALANCE
(E) TOTAL	$	

WEEK FOUR SUMMARY

CATEGORY	AMOUNT
(A) Income Total	
(B) Bills & Expenses Total	-
(C) Cash Envelopes Total	-
(D) Savings/Sinking Funds Total	-
(E) Debt Repayment Total	-
NOTE: Subtract B/C/D/E from A to determine what's left. **What's Left**	=

WEEKLY SPENDING LOG

Use the Weekly Spending Log to determine what your current spending habits are. Review the log to assess and correct impulse spending.

DATE	TRANSACTION	AMOUNT	Planned/Budgeted	Impulse Purchase
			○	○
			○	○
			○	○
			○	○
			○	○
			○	○
			○	○
			○	○
			○	○
			○	○
			○	○
			○	○
			○	○
			○	○
			○	○
			○	○
			○	○
			○	○
			○	○
			○	○
			○	○
			○	○
			○	○
			○	○
			○	○
			○	○
			○	○
			○	○
			○	○
	TOTAL	$		

Spending *Plan*

Week of:

Financial Priorities

This week's financial goal(s)

INCOME					
INCOME SOURCE	AMOUNT	Salary/Wages	Investment	Business	Side-Hustle
Rollover from previous week		☐	☐	☐	☐
		☐	☐	☐	☐
		☐	☐	☐	☐
		☐	☐	☐	☐
		☐	☐	☐	☐
		☐	☐	☐	☐
		☐	☐	☐	☐
(A) TOTAL	$				

BILLS & EXPENSES					
PAY TO	AMOUNT	Cash	Credit Card	Debit	Check
		☐	☐	☐	☐
		☐	☐	☐	☐
		☐	☐	☐	☐
		☐	☐	☐	☐
		☐	☐	☐	☐
		☐	☐	☐	☐
		☐	☐	☐	☐
		☐	☐	☐	☐
		☐	☐	☐	☐
		☐	☐	☐	☐
		☐	☐	☐	☐
		☐	☐	☐	☐
		☐	☐	☐	☐
		☐	☐	☐	☐
		☐	☐	☐	☐
(B) TOTAL	$				

CASH ENVELOPES							
CATEGORY	AMOUNT	BANKING WITHDRAWAL DENOMINATIONS					
		$1	$5	$10	$20	$50	$100
		DENOMINATION TOTAL					
(C) TOTAL	$						

SAVINGS/SINKING FUNDS

ACCOUNT	AMOUNT	Sinking Fund	Short Term	Long Term	Retirement
		☐	☐	☐	☐
		☐	☐	☐	☐
		☐	☐	☐	☐
		☐	☐	☐	☐
		☐	☐	☐	☐
		☐	☐	☐	☐
		☐	☐	☐	☐
		☐	☐	☐	☐
		☐	☐	☐	☐
		☐	☐	☐	☐
(D) TOTAL	$				

DEBT REPAYMENT

Record any payments in excess of the minimum payment due.

CREDITOR	PAYMENT	BALANCE
(E) TOTAL	$	

WEEK FIVE SUMMARY

	CATEGORY	AMOUNT
(A)	Income Total	
(B)	Bills & Expenses Total	-
(C)	Cash Envelopes Total	-
(D)	Savings/Sinking Funds Total	-
(E)	Debt Repayment Total	-
NOTE: Subtract B/C/D/E from A to determine what's left.	**What's Left**	=

WEEKLY SPENDING LOG

Use the Weekly Spending Log to determine what your current spending habits are. Review the log to assess and correct impulse spending.

DATE	TRANSACTION	AMOUNT	Planned/Budgeted	Impulse Purchase
			○	○
			○	○
			○	○
			○	○
			○	○
			○	○
			○	○
			○	○
			○	○
			○	○
			○	○
			○	○
			○	○
			○	○
			○	○
			○	○
			○	○
			○	○
			○	○
			○	○
			○	○
			○	○
			○	○
			○	○
			○	○
			○	○
			○	○
			○	○
			○	○
			○	○
	TOTAL	$		

Monthly Spending *summary*

Income

Week One	
Week Two	
Week Three	
Week Four	
Week Five	
(A) TOTAL	$

Bills and Expenses

Week One	
Week Two	
Week Three	
Week Four	
Week Five	
(B) TOTAL	$

Cash Envelopes

Week One	
Week Two	
Week Three	
Week Four	
Week Five	
(C) TOTAL	$

Savings/Sinking Funds

Week One	
Week Two	
Week Three	
Week Four	
Week Five	
(D) TOTAL	$

Debt Repayment

Week One	
Week Two	
Week Three	
Week Four	
Week Five	
(E) TOTAL	$

MONTHLY SUMMARY

(A) Income Total	
(B) Bills & Expenses Total	-
(C) Cash Envelopes Total	-
(D) Savings/SF Total	-
(E) Debt Repayment Total	-
What's Left	=

Subtract B/C/D/E from A to determine what's left.

Spending Assessment

Are there expenditures in your spending plan that can be cut or reduced? If yes, list the details below.

Impulse Spending

Review the spending log for each week, then calculate the total amount of the transactions listed as impulse purchases.

$

notes/observations

30-Day No Spend *challenge*

JAN	FEB	MAR	APR	MAY	JUN	JUL	AUG	SEP	OCT	NOV	DEC

Place a check mark on the purse which corresponds to each day that you do not make an impulse or non-essential purchase.

Total number of no-spend days

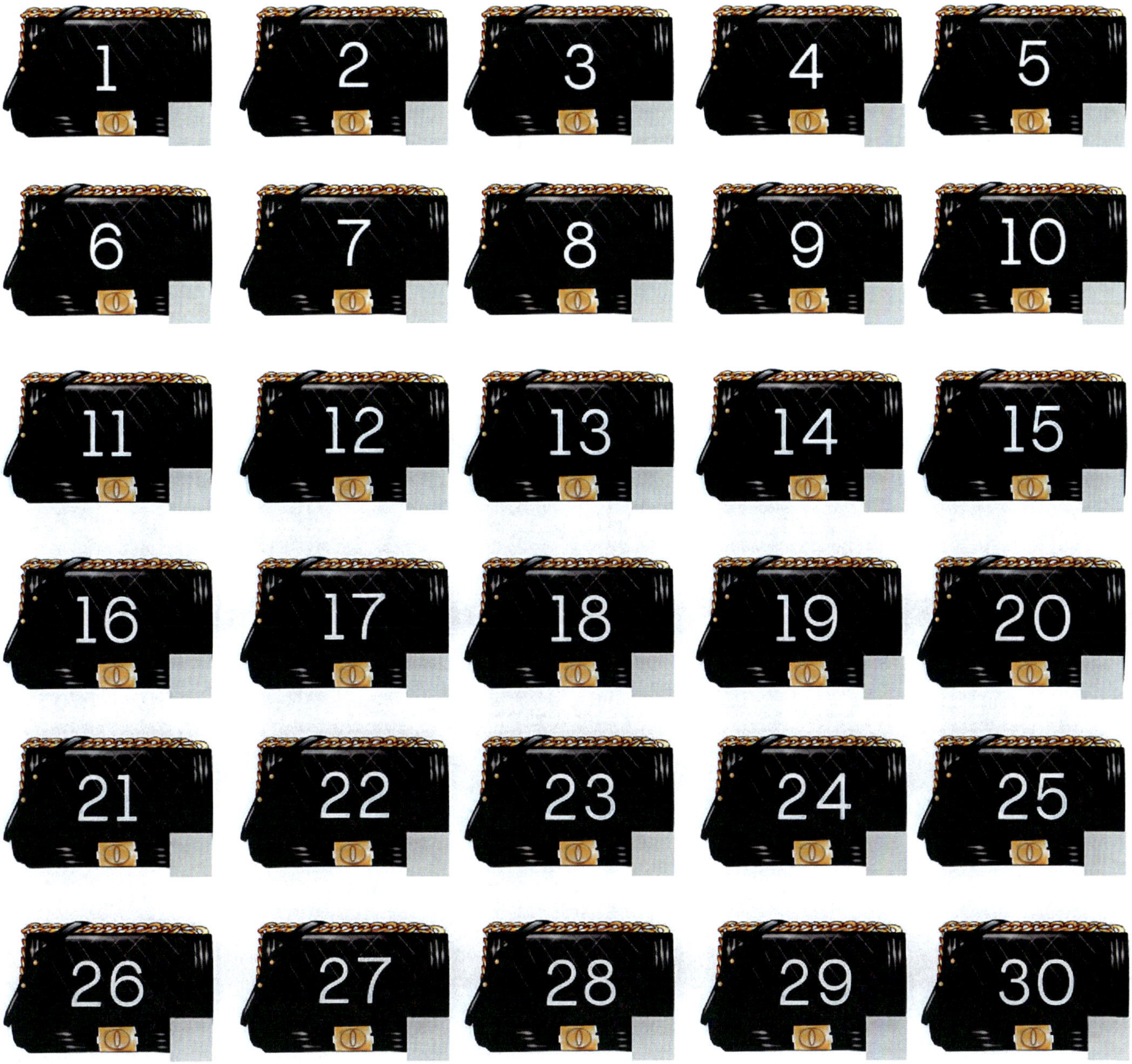

notes

Stay *focused*

"It's not how much money you make, but how much money you keep, how hard it works for you, and how many generations you keep it for."

MONTH NINE

Bill and Income *calendar*

FINANCIAL GOALS

MONDAY	TUESDAY	WEDNESDAY

JAN FEB MAR APR MAY JUN JUL AUG SEP OCT NOV DEC

THURSDAY	FRIDAY	SATURDAY	SUNDAY

Spending *Plan*

Week of:

INCOME		Salary/Wages	Investment	Business	Side-Hustle
INCOME SOURCE	AMOUNT				
Rollover from previous week		☐	☐	☐	☐
		☐	☐	☐	☐
		☐	☐	☐	☐
		☐	☐	☐	☐
		☐	☐	☐	☐
		☐	☐	☐	☐
		☐	☐	☐	☐
(A) TOTAL	$				

BILLS & EXPENSES		Cash	Credit Card	Debit	Check
PAY TO	AMOUNT				
		☐	☐	☐	☐
		☐	☐	☐	☐
		☐	☐	☐	☐
		☐	☐	☐	☐
		☐	☐	☐	☐
		☐	☐	☐	☐
		☐	☐	☐	☐
		☐	☐	☐	☐
		☐	☐	☐	☐
		☐	☐	☐	☐
		☐	☐	☐	☐
		☐	☐	☐	☐
		☐	☐	☐	☐
		☐	☐	☐	☐
		☐	☐	☐	☐
(B) TOTAL	$				

Financial Priorities

This week's financial goal(s)

CASH ENVELOPES							
CATEGORY	AMOUNT	BANKING WITHDRAWAL DENOMINATIONS					
		$1	$5	$10	$20	$50	$100
		DENOMINATION TOTAL					
(C) TOTAL	$						

SAVINGS/SINKING FUNDS

ACCOUNT	AMOUNT	Sinking Fund	Short Term	Long Term	Retirement
		☐	☐	☐	☐
		☐	☐	☐	☐
		☐	☐	☐	☐
		☐	☐	☐	☐
		☐	☐	☐	☐
		☐	☐	☐	☐
		☐	☐	☐	☐
		☐	☐	☐	☐
		☐	☐	☐	☐
		☐	☐	☐	☐
(D) TOTAL	$				

DEBT REPAYMENT

Record any payments in excess of the minimum payment due.

CREDITOR	PAYMENT	BALANCE
(E) TOTAL	$	

WEEK ONE SUMMARY

CATEGORY	AMOUNT
(A) Income Total	
(B) Bills & Expenses Total	-
(C) Cash Envelopes Total	-
(D) Savings/Sinking Funds Total	-
(E) Debt Repayment Total	-
NOTE: Subtract B/C/D/E from A to determine what's left. **What's Left**	=

WEEKLY SPENDING LOG

Use the Weekly Spending Log to determine what your current spending habits are. Review the log to assess and correct impulse spending.

DATE	TRANSACTION	AMOUNT	Planned/Budgeted	Impulse Purchase
			○	○
			○	○
			○	○
			○	○
			○	○
			○	○
			○	○
			○	○
			○	○
			○	○
			○	○
			○	○
			○	○
			○	○
			○	○
			○	○
			○	○
			○	○
			○	○
			○	○
			○	○
			○	○
			○	○
			○	○
			○	○
			○	○
			○	○
			○	○
			○	○
			○	○
TOTAL		$		

Spending *Plan*

Week of:

INCOME		Salary/Wages	Investment	Business	Side-Hustle
INCOME SOURCE	AMOUNT				
Rollover from previous week		☐	☐	☐	☐
		☐	☐	☐	☐
		☐	☐	☐	☐
		☐	☐	☐	☐
		☐	☐	☐	☐
		☐	☐	☐	☐
		☐	☐	☐	☐
(A) TOTAL	$				

BILLS & EXPENSES		Cash	Credit Card	Debit	Check
PAY TO	AMOUNT				
		☐	☐	☐	☐
		☐	☐	☐	☐
		☐	☐	☐	☐
		☐	☐	☐	☐
		☐	☐	☐	☐
		☐	☐	☐	☐
		☐	☐	☐	☐
		☐	☐	☐	☐
		☐	☐	☐	☐
		☐	☐	☐	☐
		☐	☐	☐	☐
		☐	☐	☐	☐
		☐	☐	☐	☐
		☐	☐	☐	☐
		☐	☐	☐	☐
(B) TOTAL	$				

Financial Priorities

This week's financial goal(s)

CASH ENVELOPES							
CATEGORY	AMOUNT	BANKING WITHDRAWAL DENOMINATIONS					
		$1	$5	$10	$20	$50	$100
		DENOMINATION TOTAL					
(C) TOTAL	$						

SAVINGS/SINKING FUNDS

ACCOUNT	AMOUNT	Sinking Fund	Short Term	Long Term	Retirement
		☐	☐	☐	☐
		☐	☐	☐	☐
		☐	☐	☐	☐
		☐	☐	☐	☐
		☐	☐	☐	☐
		☐	☐	☐	☐
		☐	☐	☐	☐
		☐	☐	☐	☐
		☐	☐	☐	☐
		☐	☐	☐	☐
(D) TOTAL	$				

DEBT REPAYMENT

Record any payments in excess of the minimum payment due.

CREDITOR	PAYMENT	BALANCE
(E) TOTAL	$	

WEEK TWO SUMMARY

CATEGORY	AMOUNT
(A) Income Total	
(B) Bills & Expenses Total	-
(C) Cash Envelopes Total	-
(D) Savings/Sinking Funds Total	-
(E) Debt Repayment Total	-
NOTE: Subtract B/C/D/E from A to determine what's left. **What's Left**	=

WEEKLY SPENDING LOG

Use the Weekly Spending Log to determine what your current spending habits are. Review the log to assess and correct impulse spending.

DATE	TRANSACTION	AMOUNT	Planned/Budgeted	Impulse Purchase
			○	○
			○	○
			○	○
			○	○
			○	○
			○	○
			○	○
			○	○
			○	○
			○	○
			○	○
			○	○
			○	○
			○	○
			○	○
			○	○
			○	○
			○	○
			○	○
			○	○
			○	○
			○	○
			○	○
			○	○
			○	○
			○	○
			○	○
			○	○
			○	○
			○	○
	TOTAL	$		

Spending *Plan*

Week of:

INCOME		Salary/Wages	Investment	Business	Side-Hustle
INCOME SOURCE	AMOUNT				
Rollover from previous week		☐	☐	☐	☐
		☐	☐	☐	☐
		☐	☐	☐	☐
		☐	☐	☐	☐
		☐	☐	☐	☐
		☐	☐	☐	☐
		☐	☐	☐	☐
(A) TOTAL	$				

BILLS & EXPENSES		Cash	Credit Card	Debit	Check
PAY TO	AMOUNT				
		☐	☐	☐	☐
		☐	☐	☐	☐
		☐	☐	☐	☐
		☐	☐	☐	☐
		☐	☐	☐	☐
		☐	☐	☐	☐
		☐	☐	☐	☐
		☐	☐	☐	☐
		☐	☐	☐	☐
		☐	☐	☐	☐
		☐	☐	☐	☐
		☐	☐	☐	☐
		☐	☐	☐	☐
		☐	☐	☐	☐
		☐	☐	☐	☐
(B) TOTAL	$				

Financial Priorities

This week's financial goal(s)

CASH ENVELOPES							
CATEGORY	AMOUNT	BANKING WITHDRAWAL DENOMINATIONS					
		$1	$5	$10	$20	$50	$100
		DENOMINATION TOTAL					
(C) TOTAL	$						

SAVINGS/SINKING FUNDS

ACCOUNT	AMOUNT	Sinking Fund	Short Term	Long Term	Retirement
		☐	☐	☐	☐
		☐	☐	☐	☐
		☐	☐	☐	☐
		☐	☐	☐	☐
		☐	☐	☐	☐
		☐	☐	☐	☐
		☐	☐	☐	☐
		☐	☐	☐	☐
		☐	☐	☐	☐
		☐	☐	☐	☐
(D) TOTAL	$				

DEBT REPAYMENT

Record any payments in excess of the minimum payment due.

CREDITOR	PAYMENT	BALANCE
(E) TOTAL	$	

WEEK THREE SUMMARY

CATEGORY	AMOUNT
(A) Income Total	
(B) Bills & Expenses Total	-
(C) Cash Envelopes Total	-
(D) Savings/Sinking Funds Total	-
(E) Debt Repayment Total	-
NOTE: Subtract B/C/D/E from A to determine what's left. **What's Left**	=

WEEKLY SPENDING LOG

Use the Weekly Spending Log to determine what your current spending habits are. Review the log to assess and correct impulse spending.

DATE	TRANSACTION	AMOUNT	Planned/Budgeted	Impulse Purchase
			○	○
			○	○
			○	○
			○	○
			○	○
			○	○
			○	○
			○	○
			○	○
			○	○
			○	○
			○	○
			○	○
			○	○
			○	○
			○	○
			○	○
			○	○
			○	○
			○	○
			○	○
			○	○
			○	○
			○	○
			○	○
			○	○
			○	○
			○	○
			○	○
			○	○
	TOTAL	$		

Spending *Plan*

Week of:

INCOME					
INCOME SOURCE	AMOUNT	Salary/Wages	Investment	Business	Side-Hustle
Rollover from previous week		☐	☐	☐	☐
		☐	☐	☐	☐
		☐	☐	☐	☐
		☐	☐	☐	☐
		☐	☐	☐	☐
		☐	☐	☐	☐
		☐	☐	☐	☐
(A) TOTAL	$				

BILLS & EXPENSES					
PAY TO	AMOUNT	Cash	Credit Card	Debit	Check
		☐	☐	☐	☐
		☐	☐	☐	☐
		☐	☐	☐	☐
		☐	☐	☐	☐
		☐	☐	☐	☐
		☐	☐	☐	☐
		☐	☐	☐	☐
		☐	☐	☐	☐
		☐	☐	☐	☐
		☐	☐	☐	☐
		☐	☐	☐	☐
		☐	☐	☐	☐
		☐	☐	☐	☐
		☐	☐	☐	☐
		☐	☐	☐	☐
(B) TOTAL	$				

Financial Priorities

This week's financial goal(s)

CASH ENVELOPES							
CATEGORY	AMOUNT	BANKING WITHDRAWAL DENOMINATIONS					
		$1	$5	$10	$20	$50	$100
		DENOMINATION TOTAL					
(C) TOTAL	$						

SAVINGS/SINKING FUNDS

ACCOUNT	AMOUNT	Sinking Fund	Short Term	Long Term	Retirement
		☐	☐	☐	☐
		☐	☐	☐	☐
		☐	☐	☐	☐
		☐	☐	☐	☐
		☐	☐	☐	☐
		☐	☐	☐	☐
		☐	☐	☐	☐
		☐	☐	☐	☐
		☐	☐	☐	☐
		☐	☐	☐	☐
(D) TOTAL	$				

DEBT REPAYMENT

Record any payments in excess of the minimum payment due.

CREDITOR	PAYMENT	BALANCE
(E) TOTAL	$	

WEEK FOUR SUMMARY

CATEGORY	AMOUNT
(A) Income Total	
(B) Bills & Expenses Total	-
(C) Cash Envelopes Total	-
(D) Savings/Sinking Funds Total	-
(E) Debt Repayment Total	-
NOTE: Subtract B/C/D/E from A to determine what's left. **What's Left**	=

WEEKLY SPENDING LOG

Use the Weekly Spending Log to determine what your current spending habits are. Review the log to assess and correct impulse spending.

DATE	TRANSACTION	AMOUNT	Planned/Budgeted	Impulse Purchase
			○	○
			○	○
			○	○
			○	○
			○	○
			○	○
			○	○
			○	○
			○	○
			○	○
			○	○
			○	○
			○	○
			○	○
			○	○
			○	○
			○	○
			○	○
			○	○
			○	○
			○	○
			○	○
			○	○
			○	○
			○	○
			○	○
			○	○
			○	○
			○	○
			○	○
	TOTAL	$		

Spending *Plan*

Week of:

Financial Priorities

This week's financial goal(s)

INCOME					
INCOME SOURCE	AMOUNT	Salary/Wages	Investment	Business	Side-Hustle
Rollover from previous week		☐	☐	☐	☐
		☐	☐	☐	☐
		☐	☐	☐	☐
		☐	☐	☐	☐
		☐	☐	☐	☐
		☐	☐	☐	☐
		☐	☐	☐	☐
(A) TOTAL	$				

BILLS & EXPENSES					
PAY TO	AMOUNT	Cash	Credit Card	Debit	Check
		☐	☐	☐	☐
		☐	☐	☐	☐
		☐	☐	☐	☐
		☐	☐	☐	☐
		☐	☐	☐	☐
		☐	☐	☐	☐
		☐	☐	☐	☐
		☐	☐	☐	☐
		☐	☐	☐	☐
		☐	☐	☐	☐
		☐	☐	☐	☐
		☐	☐	☐	☐
		☐	☐	☐	☐
		☐	☐	☐	☐
		☐	☐	☐	☐
(B) TOTAL	$				

CASH ENVELOPES								
CATEGORY	AMOUNT	BANKING WITHDRAWAL DENOMINATIONS						
		$1	$5	$10	$20	$50	$100
		DENOMINATION TOTAL					
(C) TOTAL	$						

SAVINGS/SINKING FUNDS

ACCOUNT	AMOUNT	Sinking Fund	Short Term	Long Term	Retirement
		☐	☐	☐	☐
		☐	☐	☐	☐
		☐	☐	☐	☐
		☐	☐	☐	☐
		☐	☐	☐	☐
		☐	☐	☐	☐
		☐	☐	☐	☐
		☐	☐	☐	☐
		☐	☐	☐	☐
		☐	☐	☐	☐
(D) TOTAL	$				

DEBT REPAYMENT

Record any payments in excess of the minimum payment due.

CREDITOR	PAYMENT	BALANCE
(E) TOTAL	$	

WEEK FIVE SUMMARY

CATEGORY	AMOUNT
(A) Income Total	
(B) Bills & Expenses Total	-
(C) Cash Envelopes Total	-
(D) Savings/Sinking Funds Total	-
(E) Debt Repayment Total	-
NOTE: Subtract B/C/D/E from A to determine what's left. **What's Left**	=

WEEKLY SPENDING LOG

Use the Weekly Spending Log to determine what your current spending habits are. Review the log to assess and correct impulse spending.

DATE	TRANSACTION	AMOUNT	Planned/Budgeted	Impulse Purchase
			○	○
			○	○
			○	○
			○	○
			○	○
			○	○
			○	○
			○	○
			○	○
			○	○
			○	○
			○	○
			○	○
			○	○
			○	○
			○	○
			○	○
			○	○
			○	○
			○	○
			○	○
			○	○
			○	○
			○	○
			○	○
			○	○
			○	○
			○	○
			○	○
	TOTAL	$		

Monthly Spending *summary*

Income	
Week One	
Week Two	
Week Three	
Week Four	
Week Five	
(A) TOTAL	$

Bills and Expenses	
Week One	
Week Two	
Week Three	
Week Four	
Week Five	
(B) TOTAL	$

Spending Assessment

Are there expenditures in your spending plan that can be cut or reduced? If yes, list the details below.

Cash Envelopes	
Week One	
Week Two	
Week Three	
Week Four	
Week Five	
(C) TOTAL	$

Savings/Sinking Funds	
Week One	
Week Two	
Week Three	
Week Four	
Week Five	
(D) TOTAL	$

Impulse Spending

Review the spending log for each week, then calculate the total amount of the transactions listed as impulse purchases.

$

Debt Repayment	
Week One	
Week Two	
Week Three	
Week Four	
Week Five	
(E) TOTAL	$

MONTHLY SUMMARY	
(A) Income Total	
(B) Bills & Expenses Total	-
(C) Cash Envelopes Total	-
(D) Savings/SF Total	-
(E) Debt Repayment Total	-
What's Left	=

Subtract B/C/D/E from A to determine what's left.

notes/observations

30-Day No Spend *challenge*

JAN	FEB	MAR	APR	MAY	JUN	JUL	AUG	SEP	OCT	NOV	DEC

Place a check mark on the purse which corresponds to each day that you do not make an impulse or non-essential purchase.

Total number of no-spend days

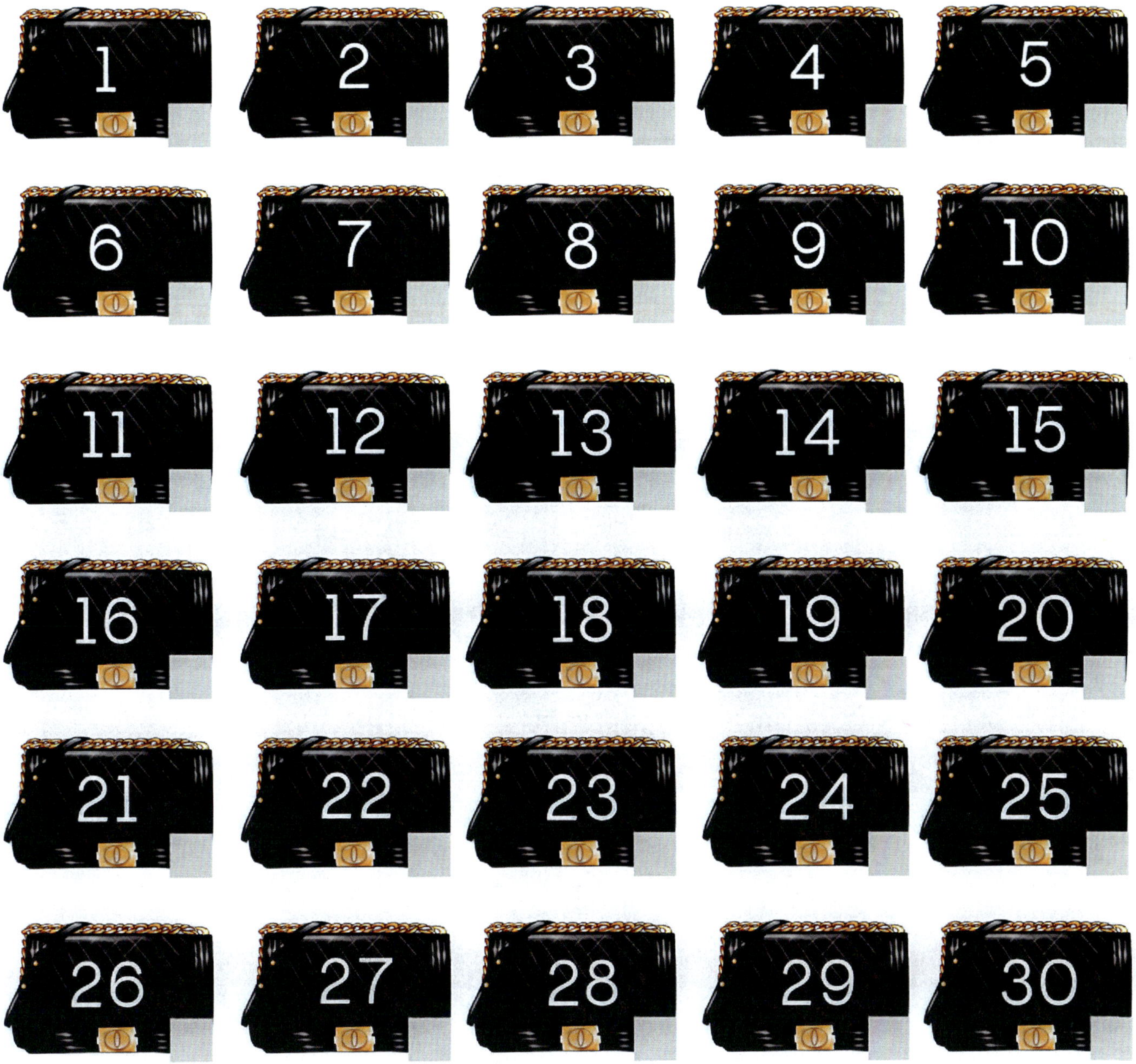

notes

Stay *focused*

"It's not how much money you make, but how much money you keep, how hard it works for you, and how many generations you keep it for."

MONTH TEN

Bill and Income *calendar*

FINANCIAL GOALS

MONDAY	TUESDAY	WEDNESDAY

JAN FEB MAR APR MAY JUN JUL AUG SEP OCT NOV DEC

THURSDAY	FRIDAY	SATURDAY	SUNDAY

Spending *Plan*

Week of:

INCOME		Salary/Wages	Investment	Business	Side-Hustle
INCOME SOURCE	AMOUNT				
Rollover from previous week		☐	☐	☐	☐
		☐	☐	☐	☐
		☐	☐	☐	☐
		☐	☐	☐	☐
		☐	☐	☐	☐
		☐	☐	☐	☐
		☐	☐	☐	☐
(A) TOTAL	$				

BILLS & EXPENSES		Cash	Credit Card	Debit	Check
PAY TO	AMOUNT				
		☐	☐	☐	☐
		☐	☐	☐	☐
		☐	☐	☐	☐
		☐	☐	☐	☐
		☐	☐	☐	☐
		☐	☐	☐	☐
		☐	☐	☐	☐
		☐	☐	☐	☐
		☐	☐	☐	☐
		☐	☐	☐	☐
		☐	☐	☐	☐
		☐	☐	☐	☐
		☐	☐	☐	☐
		☐	☐	☐	☐
		☐	☐	☐	☐
(B) TOTAL	$				

Financial Priorities

This week's financial goal(s)

CASH ENVELOPES							
CATEGORY	AMOUNT	BANKING WITHDRAWAL DENOMINATIONS					
		$1	$5	$10	$20	$50	$100
		DENOMINATION TOTAL					
(C) TOTAL	$						

SAVINGS/SINKING FUNDS

ACCOUNT	AMOUNT	Sinking Fund	Short Term	Long Term	Retirement
		☐	☐	☐	☐
		☐	☐	☐	☐
		☐	☐	☐	☐
		☐	☐	☐	☐
		☐	☐	☐	☐
		☐	☐	☐	☐
		☐	☐	☐	☐
		☐	☐	☐	☐
		☐	☐	☐	☐
		☐	☐	☐	☐
(D) TOTAL	$				

DEBT REPAYMENT

Record any payments in excess of the minimum payment due.

CREDITOR	PAYMENT	BALANCE
(E) TOTAL	$	

WEEK ONE SUMMARY

CATEGORY	AMOUNT
(A) Income Total	
(B) Bills & Expenses Total	-
(C) Cash Envelopes Total	-
(D) Savings/Sinking Funds Total	-
(E) Debt Repayment Total	-
NOTE: Subtract B/C/D/E from A to determine what's left. **What's Left**	=

WEEKLY SPENDING LOG

Use the Weekly Spending Log to determine what your current spending habits are. Review the log to assess and correct impulse spending.

DATE	TRANSACTION	AMOUNT	Planned/Budgeted	Impulse Purchase
			○	○
			○	○
			○	○
			○	○
			○	○
			○	○
			○	○
			○	○
			○	○
			○	○
			○	○
			○	○
			○	○
			○	○
			○	○
			○	○
			○	○
			○	○
			○	○
			○	○
			○	○
			○	○
			○	○
			○	○
			○	○
			○	○
			○	○
			○	○
			○	○
			○	○
	TOTAL	$		

Spending *Plan*

Week of:

INCOME		Salary/Wages	Investment	Business	Side-Hustle
INCOME SOURCE	AMOUNT				
Rollover from previous week		☐	☐	☐	☐
		☐	☐	☐	☐
		☐	☐	☐	☐
		☐	☐	☐	☐
		☐	☐	☐	☐
		☐	☐	☐	☐
		☐	☐	☐	☐
(A) TOTAL	$				

BILLS & EXPENSES		Cash	Credit Card	Debit	Check
PAY TO	AMOUNT				
		☐	☐	☐	☐
		☐	☐	☐	☐
		☐	☐	☐	☐
		☐	☐	☐	☐
		☐	☐	☐	☐
		☐	☐	☐	☐
		☐	☐	☐	☐
		☐	☐	☐	☐
		☐	☐	☐	☐
		☐	☐	☐	☐
		☐	☐	☐	☐
		☐	☐	☐	☐
		☐	☐	☐	☐
		☐	☐	☐	☐
		☐	☐	☐	☐
(B) TOTAL	$				

Financial Priorities

This week's financial goal(s)

CASH ENVELOPES							
CATEGORY	AMOUNT	BANKING WITHDRAWAL DENOMINATIONS					
		$1	$5	$10	$20	$50	$100
		DENOMINATION TOTAL					
(C) TOTAL	$						

SAVINGS/SINKING FUNDS

ACCOUNT	AMOUNT	Sinking Fund	Short Term	Long Term	Retirement
		☐	☐	☐	☐
		☐	☐	☐	☐
		☐	☐	☐	☐
		☐	☐	☐	☐
		☐	☐	☐	☐
		☐	☐	☐	☐
		☐	☐	☐	☐
		☐	☐	☐	☐
		☐	☐	☐	☐
		☐	☐	☐	☐
(D) TOTAL	$				

DEBT REPAYMENT

Record any payments in excess of the minimum payment due.

CREDITOR	PAYMENT	BALANCE
(E) TOTAL	$	

WEEK TWO SUMMARY

CATEGORY	AMOUNT
(A) Income Total	
(B) Bills & Expenses Total	-
(C) Cash Envelopes Total	-
(D) Savings/Sinking Funds Total	-
(E) Debt Repayment Total	-
NOTE: Subtract B/C/D/E from A to determine what's left. **What's Left**	=

WEEKLY SPENDING LOG

Use the Weekly Spending Log to determine what your current spending habits are. Review the log to assess and correct impulse spending.

DATE	TRANSACTION	AMOUNT	Planned/Budgeted	Impulse Purchase
			○	○
			○	○
			○	○
			○	○
			○	○
			○	○
			○	○
			○	○
			○	○
			○	○
			○	○
			○	○
			○	○
			○	○
			○	○
			○	○
			○	○
			○	○
			○	○
			○	○
			○	○
			○	○
			○	○
			○	○
			○	○
			○	○
			○	○
			○	○
			○	○
			○	○
	TOTAL	$		

Spending *Plan*

Week of:

Financial Priorities

This week's financial goal(s)

INCOME		Salary/Wages	Investment	Business	Side-Hustle
INCOME SOURCE	AMOUNT				
Rollover from previous week		☐	☐	☐	☐
		☐	☐	☐	☐
		☐	☐	☐	☐
		☐	☐	☐	☐
		☐	☐	☐	☐
		☐	☐	☐	☐
		☐	☐	☐	☐
(A) TOTAL	$				

BILLS & EXPENSES		Cash	Credit Card	Debit	Check
PAY TO	AMOUNT				
		☐	☐	☐	☐
		☐	☐	☐	☐
		☐	☐	☐	☐
		☐	☐	☐	☐
		☐	☐	☐	☐
		☐	☐	☐	☐
		☐	☐	☐	☐
		☐	☐	☐	☐
		☐	☐	☐	☐
		☐	☐	☐	☐
		☐	☐	☐	☐
		☐	☐	☐	☐
		☐	☐	☐	☐
		☐	☐	☐	☐
		☐	☐	☐	☐
(B) TOTAL	$				

CASH ENVELOPES							
CATEGORY	AMOUNT	BANKING WITHDRAWAL DENOMINATIONS					
		$1	$5	$10	$20	$50	$100
		DENOMINATION TOTAL					
(C) TOTAL	$						

SAVINGS/SINKING FUNDS

ACCOUNT	AMOUNT	Sinking Fund	Short Term	Long Term	Retirement
		☐	☐	☐	☐
		☐	☐	☐	☐
		☐	☐	☐	☐
		☐	☐	☐	☐
		☐	☐	☐	☐
		☐	☐	☐	☐
		☐	☐	☐	☐
		☐	☐	☐	☐
		☐	☐	☐	☐
		☐	☐	☐	☐
(D) TOTAL	$				

DEBT REPAYMENT

Record any payments in excess of the minimum payment due.

CREDITOR	PAYMENT	BALANCE
(E) TOTAL	$	

WEEK THREE SUMMARY

CATEGORY	AMOUNT
(A) Income Total	
(B) Bills & Expenses Total	-
(C) Cash Envelopes Total	-
(D) Savings/Sinking Funds Total	-
(E) Debt Repayment Total	-
NOTE: Subtract B/C/D/E from A to determine what's left. **What's Left**	=

WEEKLY SPENDING LOG

Use the Weekly Spending Log to determine what your current spending habits are. Review the log to assess and correct impulse spending.

DATE	TRANSACTION	AMOUNT	Planned/Budgeted	Impulse Purchase
			○	○
			○	○
			○	○
			○	○
			○	○
			○	○
			○	○
			○	○
			○	○
			○	○
			○	○
			○	○
			○	○
			○	○
			○	○
			○	○
			○	○
			○	○
			○	○
			○	○
			○	○
			○	○
			○	○
			○	○
			○	○
			○	○
			○	○
			○	○
			○	○
			○	○
	TOTAL	$		

Spending *Plan*

Week of:

INCOME					
INCOME SOURCE	AMOUNT	Salary/Wages	Investment	Business	Side-Hustle
Rollover from previous week		☐	☐	☐	☐
		☐	☐	☐	☐
		☐	☐	☐	☐
		☐	☐	☐	☐
		☐	☐	☐	☐
		☐	☐	☐	☐
		☐	☐	☐	☐
(A) TOTAL	$				

BILLS & EXPENSES					
PAY TO	AMOUNT	Cash	Credit Card	Debit	Check
		☐	☐	☐	☐
		☐	☐	☐	☐
		☐	☐	☐	☐
		☐	☐	☐	☐
		☐	☐	☐	☐
		☐	☐	☐	☐
		☐	☐	☐	☐
		☐	☐	☐	☐
		☐	☐	☐	☐
		☐	☐	☐	☐
		☐	☐	☐	☐
		☐	☐	☐	☐
		☐	☐	☐	☐
		☐	☐	☐	☐
		☐	☐	☐	☐
(B) TOTAL	$				

Financial Priorities

This week's financial goal(s)

CASH ENVELOPES							
CATEGORY	AMOUNT	BANKING WITHDRAWAL DENOMINATIONS					
		$1	$5	$10	$20	$50	$100
		DENOMINATION TOTAL					
(C) TOTAL	$						

SAVINGS/SINKING FUNDS

ACCOUNT	AMOUNT	Sinking Fund	Short Term	Long Term	Retirement
		☐	☐	☐	☐
		☐	☐	☐	☐
		☐	☐	☐	☐
		☐	☐	☐	☐
		☐	☐	☐	☐
		☐	☐	☐	☐
		☐	☐	☐	☐
		☐	☐	☐	☐
		☐	☐	☐	☐
		☐	☐	☐	☐
(D) TOTAL	$				

DEBT REPAYMENT

Record any payments in excess of the minimum payment due.

CREDITOR	PAYMENT	BALANCE
(E) TOTAL	$	

WEEK FOUR SUMMARY

CATEGORY	AMOUNT
(A) Income Total	
(B) Bills & Expenses Total	-
(C) Cash Envelopes Total	-
(D) Savings/Sinking Funds Total	-
(E) Debt Repayment Total	-
NOTE: Subtract B/C/D/E from A to determine what's left. **What's Left**	=

WEEKLY SPENDING LOG

Use the Weekly Spending Log to determine what your current spending habits are. Review the log to assess and correct impulse spending.

DATE	TRANSACTION	AMOUNT	Planned/Budgeted	Impulse Purchase
			○	○
			○	○
			○	○
			○	○
			○	○
			○	○
			○	○
			○	○
			○	○
			○	○
			○	○
			○	○
			○	○
			○	○
			○	○
			○	○
			○	○
			○	○
			○	○
			○	○
			○	○
			○	○
			○	○
			○	○
			○	○
			○	○
			○	○
			○	○
			○	○
			○	○
	TOTAL	$		

Spending *Plan*

Week of:

INCOME					
INCOME SOURCE	AMOUNT	Salary/Wages	Investment	Business	Side-Hustle
Rollover from previous week		☐	☐	☐	☐
		☐	☐	☐	☐
		☐	☐	☐	☐
		☐	☐	☐	☐
		☐	☐	☐	☐
		☐	☐	☐	☐
		☐	☐	☐	☐
(A) TOTAL	$				

BILLS & EXPENSES					
PAY TO	AMOUNT	Cash	Credit Card	Debit	Check
		☐	☐	☐	☐
		☐	☐	☐	☐
		☐	☐	☐	☐
		☐	☐	☐	☐
		☐	☐	☐	☐
		☐	☐	☐	☐
		☐	☐	☐	☐
		☐	☐	☐	☐
		☐	☐	☐	☐
		☐	☐	☐	☐
		☐	☐	☐	☐
		☐	☐	☐	☐
		☐	☐	☐	☐
		☐	☐	☐	☐
		☐	☐	☐	☐
(B) TOTAL	$				

Financial Priorities

This week's financial goal(s)

CASH ENVELOPES							
CATEGORY	AMOUNT	BANKING WITHDRAWAL DENOMINATIONS					
		$1	$5	$10	$20	$50	$100
		DENOMINATION TOTAL					
(C) TOTAL	$						

SAVINGS/SINKING FUNDS

ACCOUNT	AMOUNT	Sinking Fund	Short Term	Long Term	Retirement
		☐	☐	☐	☐
		☐	☐	☐	☐
		☐	☐	☐	☐
		☐	☐	☐	☐
		☐	☐	☐	☐
		☐	☐	☐	☐
		☐	☐	☐	☐
		☐	☐	☐	☐
		☐	☐	☐	☐
		☐	☐	☐	☐
(D) TOTAL	$				

DEBT REPAYMENT

Record any payments in excess of the minimum payment due.

CREDITOR	PAYMENT	BALANCE
(E) TOTAL	$	

WEEK FIVE SUMMARY

CATEGORY	AMOUNT
(A) Income Total	
(B) Bills & Expenses Total	-
(C) Cash Envelopes Total	-
(D) Savings/Sinking Funds Total	-
(E) Debt Repayment Total	-
NOTE: Subtract B/C/D/E from A to determine what's left. **What's Left**	=

WEEKLY SPENDING LOG

Use the Weekly Spending Log to determine what your current spending habits are. Review the log to assess and correct impulse spending.

DATE	TRANSACTION	AMOUNT	Planned/Budgeted	Impulse Purchase
			○	○
			○	○
			○	○
			○	○
			○	○
			○	○
			○	○
			○	○
			○	○
			○	○
			○	○
			○	○
			○	○
			○	○
			○	○
			○	○
			○	○
			○	○
			○	○
			○	○
			○	○
			○	○
			○	○
			○	○
			○	○
			○	○
			○	○
			○	○
			○	○
			○	○
	TOTAL	$		

Monthly Spending *summary*

Income	
Week One	
Week Two	
Week Three	
Week Four	
Week Five	
(A) TOTAL	$

Bills and Expenses	
Week One	
Week Two	
Week Three	
Week Four	
Week Five	
(B) TOTAL	$

Cash Envelopes	
Week One	
Week Two	
Week Three	
Week Four	
Week Five	
(C) TOTAL	$

Savings/Sinking Funds	
Week One	
Week Two	
Week Three	
Week Four	
Week Five	
(D) TOTAL	$

Debt Repayment	
Week One	
Week Two	
Week Three	
Week Four	
Week Five	
(E) TOTAL	$

MONTHLY SUMMARY	
(A) Income Total	
(B) Bills & Expenses Total	-
(C) Cash Envelopes Total	-
(D) Savings/SF Total	-
(E) Debt Repayment Total	-
What's Left	=

Subtract B/C/D/E from A to determine what's left.

Spending Assessment

Are there expenditures in your spending plan that can be cut or reduced? If yes, list the details below.

Impulse Spending

Review the spending log for each week, then calculate the total amount of the transactions listed as impulse purchases.

$

notes/observations

30-Day No Spend *challenge*

JAN	FEB	MAR	APR	MAY	JUN	JUL	AUG	SEP	OCT	NOV	DEC

Place a check mark on the purse which corresponds to each day that you do not make an impulse or non-essential purchase.

Total number of no-spend days

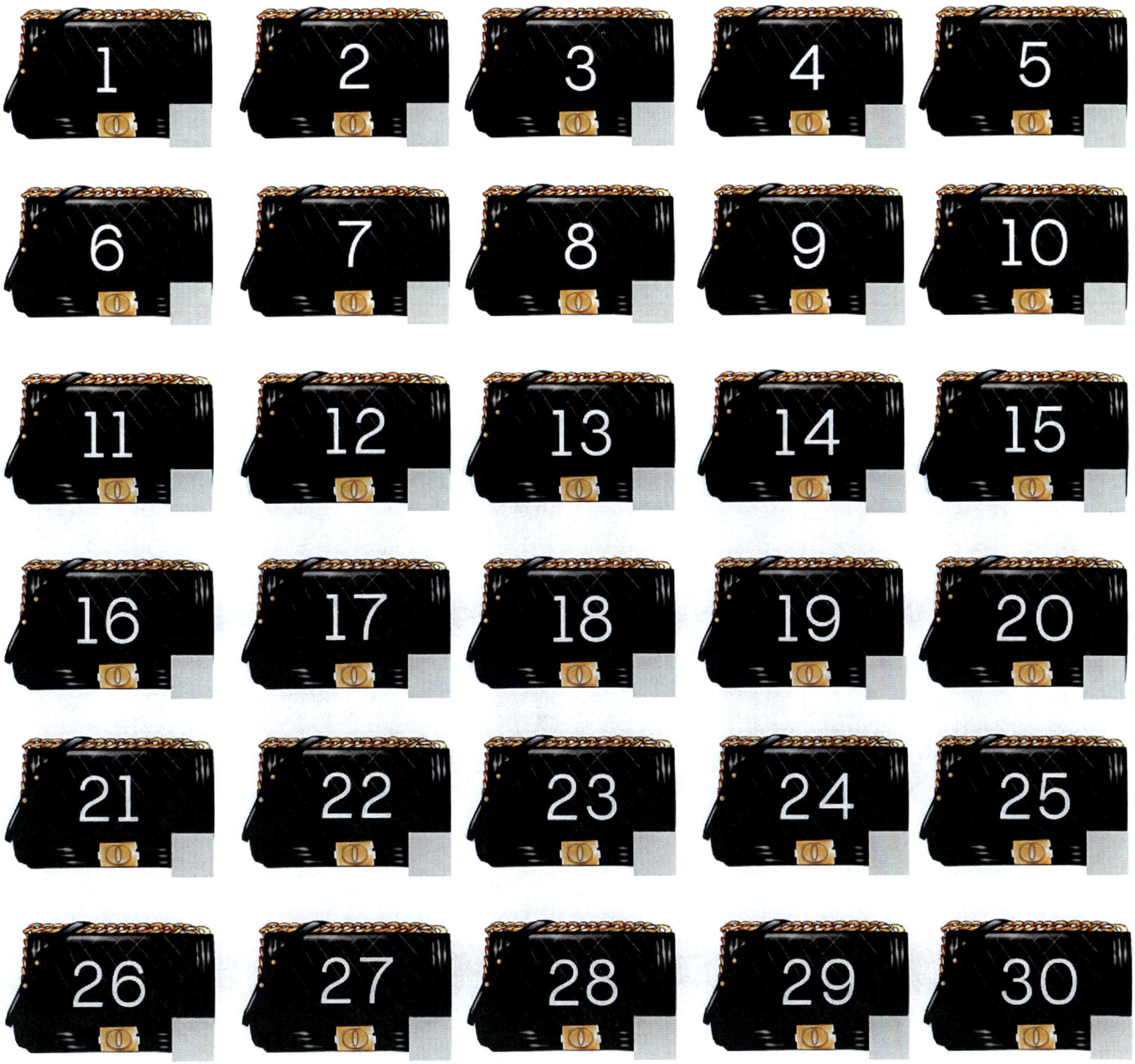

notes

Stay *focused*

"It's not how much money you make, but how much money you keep, how hard it works for you, and how many generations you keep it for."

MONTH ELEVEN

Bill and Income *calendar*

FINANCIAL GOALS

MONDAY	TUESDAY	WEDNESDAY

JAN FEB MAR APR MAY JUN JUL AUG SEP OCT NOV DEC

THURSDAY	FRIDAY	SATURDAY	SUNDAY

Spending *Plan*

Week of:

INCOME		Salary/Wages	Investment	Business	Side-Hustle
INCOME SOURCE	AMOUNT				
Rollover from previous week		☐	☐	☐	☐
		☐	☐	☐	☐
		☐	☐	☐	☐
		☐	☐	☐	☐
		☐	☐	☐	☐
		☐	☐	☐	☐
		☐	☐	☐	☐
(A) TOTAL	$				

BILLS & EXPENSES		Cash	Credit Card	Debit	Check
PAY TO	AMOUNT				
		☐	☐	☐	☐
		☐	☐	☐	☐
		☐	☐	☐	☐
		☐	☐	☐	☐
		☐	☐	☐	☐
		☐	☐	☐	☐
		☐	☐	☐	☐
		☐	☐	☐	☐
		☐	☐	☐	☐
		☐	☐	☐	☐
		☐	☐	☐	☐
		☐	☐	☐	☐
		☐	☐	☐	☐
		☐	☐	☐	☐
		☐	☐	☐	☐
(B) TOTAL	$				

Financial Priorities

This week's financial goal(s)

CASH ENVELOPES							
CATEGORY	AMOUNT	BANKING WITHDRAWAL DENOMINATIONS					
		$1	$5	$10	$20	$50	$100
		DENOMINATION TOTAL					
(C) TOTAL	$						

SAVINGS/SINKING FUNDS

ACCOUNT	AMOUNT	Sinking Fund	Short Term	Long Term	Retirement
		☐	☐	☐	☐
		☐	☐	☐	☐
		☐	☐	☐	☐
		☐	☐	☐	☐
		☐	☐	☐	☐
		☐	☐	☐	☐
		☐	☐	☐	☐
		☐	☐	☐	☐
		☐	☐	☐	☐
		☐	☐	☐	☐
(D) TOTAL	$				

DEBT REPAYMENT

Record any payments in excess of the minimum payment due.

CREDITOR	PAYMENT	BALANCE
(E) TOTAL	$	

WEEK ONE SUMMARY

CATEGORY	AMOUNT
(A) Income Total	
(B) Bills & Expenses Total	-
(C) Cash Envelopes Total	-
(D) Savings/Sinking Funds Total	-
(E) Debt Repayment Total	-
NOTE: Subtract B/C/D/E from A to determine what's left. **What's Left**	=

WEEKLY SPENDING LOG

Use the Weekly Spending Log to determine what your current spending habits are. Review the log to assess and correct impulse spending.

DATE	TRANSACTION	AMOUNT	Planned/Budgeted	Impulse Purchase
			○	○
			○	○
			○	○
			○	○
			○	○
			○	○
			○	○
			○	○
			○	○
			○	○
			○	○
			○	○
			○	○
			○	○
			○	○
			○	○
			○	○
			○	○
			○	○
			○	○
			○	○
			○	○
			○	○
			○	○
			○	○
			○	○
			○	○
			○	○
			○	○
			○	○
	TOTAL	$		

Spending *Plan*

Week of:

INCOME

INCOME SOURCE	AMOUNT	Salary/Wages	Investment	Business	Side-Hustle
Rollover from previous week		☐	☐	☐	☐
		☐	☐	☐	☐
		☐	☐	☐	☐
		☐	☐	☐	☐
		☐	☐	☐	☐
		☐	☐	☐	☐
		☐	☐	☐	☐
(A) TOTAL	$				

BILLS & EXPENSES

PAY TO	AMOUNT	Cash	Credit Card	Debit	Check
		☐	☐	☐	☐
		☐	☐	☐	☐
		☐	☐	☐	☐
		☐	☐	☐	☐
		☐	☐	☐	☐
		☐	☐	☐	☐
		☐	☐	☐	☐
		☐	☐	☐	☐
		☐	☐	☐	☐
		☐	☐	☐	☐
		☐	☐	☐	☐
		☐	☐	☐	☐
		☐	☐	☐	☐
		☐	☐	☐	☐
		☐	☐	☐	☐
(B) TOTAL	$				

Financial Priorities

This week's financial goal(s)

CASH ENVELOPES

CATEGORY	AMOUNT	BANKING WITHDRAWAL DENOMINATIONS					
		$1	$5	$10	$20	$50	$100
		DENOMINATION TOTAL					
(C) TOTAL	$						

SAVINGS/SINKING FUNDS

ACCOUNT	AMOUNT	Sinking Fund	Short Term	Long Term	Retirement
		☐	☐	☐	☐
		☐	☐	☐	☐
		☐	☐	☐	☐
		☐	☐	☐	☐
		☐	☐	☐	☐
		☐	☐	☐	☐
		☐	☐	☐	☐
		☐	☐	☐	☐
		☐	☐	☐	☐
		☐	☐	☐	☐
(D) TOTAL	$				

DEBT REPAYMENT

Record any payments in excess of the minimum payment due.

CREDITOR	PAYMENT	BALANCE
(E) TOTAL	$	

WEEK TWO SUMMARY

CATEGORY	AMOUNT
(A) Income Total	
(B) Bills & Expenses Total	-
(C) Cash Envelopes Total	-
(D) Savings/Sinking Funds Total	-
(E) Debt Repayment Total	-
NOTE: Subtract B/C/D/E from A to determine what's left. **What's Left**	=

WEEKLY SPENDING LOG

Use the Weekly Spending Log to determine what your current spending habits are. Review the log to assess and correct impulse spending.

DATE	TRANSACTION	AMOUNT	Planned/Budgeted	Impulse Purchase
			○	○
			○	○
			○	○
			○	○
			○	○
			○	○
			○	○
			○	○
			○	○
			○	○
			○	○
			○	○
			○	○
			○	○
			○	○
			○	○
			○	○
			○	○
			○	○
			○	○
			○	○
			○	○
			○	○
			○	○
			○	○
			○	○
			○	○
			○	○
			○	○
			○	○
	TOTAL	$		

Spending *Plan*

Week of:

INCOME		Salary/Wages	Investment	Business	Side-Hustle
INCOME SOURCE	AMOUNT				
Rollover from previous week		☐	☐	☐	☐
		☐	☐	☐	☐
		☐	☐	☐	☐
		☐	☐	☐	☐
		☐	☐	☐	☐
		☐	☐	☐	☐
		☐	☐	☐	☐
(A) TOTAL	$				

BILLS & EXPENSES		Cash	Credit Card	Debit	Check
PAY TO	AMOUNT				
		☐	☐	☐	☐
		☐	☐	☐	☐
		☐	☐	☐	☐
		☐	☐	☐	☐
		☐	☐	☐	☐
		☐	☐	☐	☐
		☐	☐	☐	☐
		☐	☐	☐	☐
		☐	☐	☐	☐
		☐	☐	☐	☐
		☐	☐	☐	☐
		☐	☐	☐	☐
		☐	☐	☐	☐
		☐	☐	☐	☐
		☐	☐	☐	☐
(B) TOTAL	$				

Financial Priorities

This week's financial goal(s)

CASH ENVELOPES							
CATEGORY	AMOUNT	BANKING WITHDRAWAL DENOMINATIONS					
		$1	$5	$10	$20	$50	$100
		DENOMINATION TOTAL					
(C) TOTAL	$						

SAVINGS/SINKING FUNDS

ACCOUNT	AMOUNT	Sinking Fund	Short Term	Long Term	Retirement
		☐	☐	☐	☐
		☐	☐	☐	☐
		☐	☐	☐	☐
		☐	☐	☐	☐
		☐	☐	☐	☐
		☐	☐	☐	☐
		☐	☐	☐	☐
		☐	☐	☐	☐
		☐	☐	☐	☐
		☐	☐	☐	☐
(D) TOTAL	$				

DEBT REPAYMENT

Record any payments in excess of the minimum payment due.

CREDITOR	PAYMENT	BALANCE
(E) TOTAL	$	

WEEK THREE SUMMARY

CATEGORY	AMOUNT
(A) Income Total	
(B) Bills & Expenses Total	-
(C) Cash Envelopes Total	-
(D) Savings/Sinking Funds Total	-
(E) Debt Repayment Total	-
NOTE: Subtract B/C/D/E from A to determine what's left. **What's Left**	=

WEEKLY SPENDING LOG

Use the Weekly Spending Log to determine what your current spending habits are. Review the log to assess and correct impulse spending.

DATE	TRANSACTION	AMOUNT	Planned/Budgeted	Impulse Purchase
			○	○
			○	○
			○	○
			○	○
			○	○
			○	○
			○	○
			○	○
			○	○
			○	○
			○	○
			○	○
			○	○
			○	○
			○	○
			○	○
			○	○
			○	○
			○	○
			○	○
			○	○
			○	○
			○	○
			○	○
			○	○
			○	○
			○	○
			○	○
			○	○
			○	○
	TOTAL	$		

Spending *Plan*

Week of:

INCOME		Salary/Wages	Investment	Business	Side-Hustle
INCOME SOURCE	AMOUNT				
Rollover from previous week		☐	☐	☐	☐
		☐	☐	☐	☐
		☐	☐	☐	☐
		☐	☐	☐	☐
		☐	☐	☐	☐
		☐	☐	☐	☐
		☐	☐	☐	☐
(A) TOTAL	$				

BILLS & EXPENSES		Cash	Credit Card	Debit	Check
PAY TO	AMOUNT				
		☐	☐	☐	☐
		☐	☐	☐	☐
		☐	☐	☐	☐
		☐	☐	☐	☐
		☐	☐	☐	☐
		☐	☐	☐	☐
		☐	☐	☐	☐
		☐	☐	☐	☐
		☐	☐	☐	☐
		☐	☐	☐	☐
		☐	☐	☐	☐
		☐	☐	☐	☐
		☐	☐	☐	☐
		☐	☐	☐	☐
		☐	☐	☐	☐
(B) TOTAL	$				

Financial Priorities

This week's financial goal(s)

CASH ENVELOPES							
CATEGORY	AMOUNT	BANKING WITHDRAWAL DENOMINATIONS					
		$1	$5	$10	$20	$50	$100
		DENOMINATION TOTAL					
(C) TOTAL	$						

SAVINGS/SINKING FUNDS

ACCOUNT	AMOUNT	Sinking Fund	Short Term	Long Term	Retirement
		☐	☐	☐	☐
		☐	☐	☐	☐
		☐	☐	☐	☐
		☐	☐	☐	☐
		☐	☐	☐	☐
		☐	☐	☐	☐
		☐	☐	☐	☐
		☐	☐	☐	☐
		☐	☐	☐	☐
		☐	☐	☐	☐
(D) TOTAL	$				

DEBT REPAYMENT

Record any payments in excess of the minimum payment due.

CREDITOR	PAYMENT	BALANCE
(E) TOTAL	$	

WEEK FOUR SUMMARY

CATEGORY	AMOUNT
(A) Income Total	
(B) Bills & Expenses Total	-
(C) Cash Envelopes Total	-
(D) Savings/Sinking Funds Total	-
(E) Debt Repayment Total	-
NOTE: Subtract B/C/D/E from A to determine what's left. **What's Left**	=

WEEKLY SPENDING LOG

Use the Weekly Spending Log to determine what your current spending habits are. Review the log to assess and correct impulse spending.

DATE	TRANSACTION	AMOUNT	Planned/Budgeted	Impulse Purchase
			○	○
			○	○
			○	○
			○	○
			○	○
			○	○
			○	○
			○	○
			○	○
			○	○
			○	○
			○	○
			○	○
			○	○
			○	○
			○	○
			○	○
			○	○
			○	○
			○	○
			○	○
			○	○
			○	○
			○	○
			○	○
			○	○
			○	○
			○	○
			○	○
			○	○
	TOTAL	$		

Spending Plan

Week of:

INCOME		Salary/Wages	Investment	Business	Side-Hustle
INCOME SOURCE	AMOUNT				
Rollover from previous week		☐	☐	☐	☐
		☐	☐	☐	☐
		☐	☐	☐	☐
		☐	☐	☐	☐
		☐	☐	☐	☐
		☐	☐	☐	☐
		☐	☐	☐	☐
(A) TOTAL	$				

BILLS & EXPENSES		Cash	Credit Card	Debit	Check
PAY TO	AMOUNT				
		☐	☐	☐	☐
		☐	☐	☐	☐
		☐	☐	☐	☐
		☐	☐	☐	☐
		☐	☐	☐	☐
		☐	☐	☐	☐
		☐	☐	☐	☐
		☐	☐	☐	☐
		☐	☐	☐	☐
		☐	☐	☐	☐
		☐	☐	☐	☐
		☐	☐	☐	☐
		☐	☐	☐	☐
		☐	☐	☐	☐
		☐	☐	☐	☐
(B) TOTAL	$				

Financial Priorities

This week's financial goal(s)

CASH ENVELOPES							
CATEGORY	AMOUNT	BANKING WITHDRAWAL DENOMINATIONS					
		$1	$5	$10	$20	$50	$100
		DENOMINATION TOTAL					
(C) TOTAL	$						

SAVINGS/SINKING FUNDS

ACCOUNT	AMOUNT	Sinking Fund	Short Term	Long Term	Retirement
		☐	☐	☐	☐
		☐	☐	☐	☐
		☐	☐	☐	☐
		☐	☐	☐	☐
		☐	☐	☐	☐
		☐	☐	☐	☐
		☐	☐	☐	☐
		☐	☐	☐	☐
		☐	☐	☐	☐
		☐	☐	☐	☐
(D) TOTAL	$				

DEBT REPAYMENT

Record any payments in excess of the minimum payment due.

CREDITOR	PAYMENT	BALANCE
(E) TOTAL	$	

WEEK FIVE SUMMARY

CATEGORY	AMOUNT
(A) Income Total	
(B) Bills & Expenses Total	-
(C) Cash Envelopes Total	-
(D) Savings/Sinking Funds Total	-
(E) Debt Repayment Total	-
NOTE: Subtract B/C/D/E from A to determine what's left. **What's Left**	=

WEEKLY SPENDING LOG

Use the Weekly Spending Log to determine what your current spending habits are. Review the log to assess and correct impulse spending.

DATE	TRANSACTION	AMOUNT	Planned/Budgeted	Impulse Purchase
			○	○
			○	○
			○	○
			○	○
			○	○
			○	○
			○	○
			○	○
			○	○
			○	○
			○	○
			○	○
			○	○
			○	○
			○	○
			○	○
			○	○
			○	○
			○	○
			○	○
			○	○
			○	○
			○	○
			○	○
			○	○
			○	○
			○	○
			○	○
			○	○
			○	○
			○	○
TOTAL		$		

Monthly Spending *summary*

Income	
Week One	
Week Two	
Week Three	
Week Four	
Week Five	
(A) TOTAL	$

Bills and Expenses	
Week One	
Week Two	
Week Three	
Week Four	
Week Five	
(B) TOTAL	$

Cash Envelopes	
Week One	
Week Two	
Week Three	
Week Four	
Week Five	
(C) TOTAL	$

Savings/Sinking Funds	
Week One	
Week Two	
Week Three	
Week Four	
Week Five	
(D) TOTAL	$

Debt Repayment	
Week One	
Week Two	
Week Three	
Week Four	
Week Five	
(E) TOTAL	$

MONTHLY SUMMARY	
(A) Income Total	
(B) Bills & Expenses Total	-
(C) Cash Envelopes Total	-
(D) Savings/SF Total	-
(E) Debt Repayment Total	-
What's Left	=

Subtract B/C/D/E from A to determine what's left.

Spending Assessment

Are there expenditures in your spending plan that can be cut or reduced? If yes, list the details below.

Impulse Spending

Review the spending log for each week, then calculate the total amount of the transactions listed as impulse purchases.

$

notes/observations

30-Day No Spend *challenge*

JAN	FEB	MAR	APR	MAY	JUN	JUL	AUG	SEP	OCT	NOV	DEC

Place a check mark on the purse which corresponds to each day that you do not make an impulse or non-essential purchase.

Total number of no-spend days

notes

Stay *focused*

"It's not how much money you make, but how much money you keep, how hard it works for you, and how many generations you keep it for."

MONTH TWELVE

Bill and Income *calendar*

FINANCIAL GOALS

MONDAY	TUESDAY	WEDNESDAY

JAN FEB MAR APR MAY JUN JUL AUG SEP OCT NOV DEC

THURSDAY	FRIDAY	SATURDAY	SUNDAY

Spending *Plan*

Week of:

INCOME		Salary/Wages	Investment	Business	Side-Hustle
INCOME SOURCE	AMOUNT				
Rollover from previous week		☐	☐	☐	☐
		☐	☐	☐	☐
		☐	☐	☐	☐
		☐	☐	☐	☐
		☐	☐	☐	☐
		☐	☐	☐	☐
		☐	☐	☐	☐
(A) TOTAL	$				

BILLS & EXPENSES		Cash	Credit Card	Debit	Check
PAY TO	AMOUNT				
		☐	☐	☐	☐
		☐	☐	☐	☐
		☐	☐	☐	☐
		☐	☐	☐	☐
		☐	☐	☐	☐
		☐	☐	☐	☐
		☐	☐	☐	☐
		☐	☐	☐	☐
		☐	☐	☐	☐
		☐	☐	☐	☐
		☐	☐	☐	☐
		☐	☐	☐	☐
		☐	☐	☐	☐
		☐	☐	☐	☐
		☐	☐	☐	☐
(B) TOTAL	$				

Financial Priorities

This week's financial goal(s)

CASH ENVELOPES							
CATEGORY	AMOUNT	BANKING WITHDRAWAL DENOMINATIONS					
		$1	$5	$10	$20	$50	$100
		DENOMINATION TOTAL					
(C) TOTAL	$						

SAVINGS/SINKING FUNDS

ACCOUNT	AMOUNT	Sinking Fund	Short Term	Long Term	Retirement
		☐	☐	☐	☐
		☐	☐	☐	☐
		☐	☐	☐	☐
		☐	☐	☐	☐
		☐	☐	☐	☐
		☐	☐	☐	☐
		☐	☐	☐	☐
		☐	☐	☐	☐
		☐	☐	☐	☐
		☐	☐	☐	☐
(D) TOTAL	$				

DEBT REPAYMENT

Record any payments in excess of the minimum payment due.

CREDITOR	PAYMENT	BALANCE
(E) TOTAL	$	

WEEK ONE SUMMARY

CATEGORY	AMOUNT
(A) Income Total	
(B) Bills & Expenses Total	-
(C) Cash Envelopes Total	-
(D) Savings/Sinking Funds Total	-
(E) Debt Repayment Total	-
NOTE: Subtract B/C/D/E from A to determine what's left. **What's Left**	=

WEEKLY SPENDING LOG

Use the Weekly Spending Log to determine what your current spending habits are. Review the log to assess and correct impulse spending.

DATE	TRANSACTION	AMOUNT	Planned/Budgeted	Impulse Purchase
			○	○
			○	○
			○	○
			○	○
			○	○
			○	○
			○	○
			○	○
			○	○
			○	○
			○	○
			○	○
			○	○
			○	○
			○	○
			○	○
			○	○
			○	○
			○	○
			○	○
			○	○
			○	○
			○	○
			○	○
			○	○
			○	○
			○	○
			○	○
			○	○
			○	○
			○	○
TOTAL		$		

Spending Plan

Week of:

Financial Priorities

This week's financial goal(s)

INCOME		Salary/Wages	Investment	Business	Side-Hustle
INCOME SOURCE	AMOUNT				
Rollover from previous week		☐	☐	☐	☐
		☐	☐	☐	☐
		☐	☐	☐	☐
		☐	☐	☐	☐
		☐	☐	☐	☐
		☐	☐	☐	☐
		☐	☐	☐	☐
(A) TOTAL	$				

BILLS & EXPENSES		Cash	Credit Card	Debit	Check
PAY TO	AMOUNT				
		☐	☐	☐	☐
		☐	☐	☐	☐
		☐	☐	☐	☐
		☐	☐	☐	☐
		☐	☐	☐	☐
		☐	☐	☐	☐
		☐	☐	☐	☐
		☐	☐	☐	☐
		☐	☐	☐	☐
		☐	☐	☐	☐
		☐	☐	☐	☐
		☐	☐	☐	☐
		☐	☐	☐	☐
		☐	☐	☐	☐
		☐	☐	☐	☐
(B) TOTAL	$				

CASH ENVELOPES							
CATEGORY	AMOUNT	BANKING WITHDRAWAL DENOMINATIONS					
		$1	$5	$10	$20	$50	$100
		DENOMINATION TOTAL					
(C) TOTAL	$						

SAVINGS/SINKING FUNDS

ACCOUNT	AMOUNT	Sinking Fund	Short Term	Long Term	Retirement
		☐	☐	☐	☐
		☐	☐	☐	☐
		☐	☐	☐	☐
		☐	☐	☐	☐
		☐	☐	☐	☐
		☐	☐	☐	☐
		☐	☐	☐	☐
		☐	☐	☐	☐
		☐	☐	☐	☐
		☐	☐	☐	☐
(D) TOTAL	$				

DEBT REPAYMENT

Record any payments in excess of the minimum payment due.

CREDITOR	PAYMENT	BALANCE
(E) TOTAL	$	

WEEK TWO SUMMARY

CATEGORY	AMOUNT
(A) Income Total	
(B) Bills & Expenses Total	-
(C) Cash Envelopes Total	-
(D) Savings/Sinking Funds Total	-
(E) Debt Repayment Total	-
NOTE: Subtract B/C/D/E from A to determine what's left. **What's Left**	=

WEEKLY SPENDING LOG

Use the Weekly Spending Log to determine what your current spending habits are. Review the log to assess and correct impulse spending.

DATE	TRANSACTION	AMOUNT	Planned/Budgeted	Impulse Purchase
			○	○
			○	○
			○	○
			○	○
			○	○
			○	○
			○	○
			○	○
			○	○
			○	○
			○	○
			○	○
			○	○
			○	○
			○	○
			○	○
			○	○
			○	○
			○	○
			○	○
			○	○
			○	○
			○	○
			○	○
			○	○
			○	○
			○	○
			○	○
			○	○
			○	○
	TOTAL	$		

Spending *Plan*

Week of:

INCOME		Salary/Wages	Investment	Business	Side-Hustle
INCOME SOURCE	AMOUNT				
Rollover from previous week		☐	☐	☐	☐
		☐	☐	☐	☐
		☐	☐	☐	☐
		☐	☐	☐	☐
		☐	☐	☐	☐
		☐	☐	☐	☐
		☐	☐	☐	☐
(A) TOTAL	$				

BILLS & EXPENSES		Cash	Credit Card	Debit	Check
PAY TO	AMOUNT				
		☐	☐	☐	☐
		☐	☐	☐	☐
		☐	☐	☐	☐
		☐	☐	☐	☐
		☐	☐	☐	☐
		☐	☐	☐	☐
		☐	☐	☐	☐
		☐	☐	☐	☐
		☐	☐	☐	☐
		☐	☐	☐	☐
		☐	☐	☐	☐
		☐	☐	☐	☐
		☐	☐	☐	☐
		☐	☐	☐	☐
		☐	☐	☐	☐
(B) TOTAL	$				

Financial Priorities

This week's financial goal(s)

CASH ENVELOPES							
CATEGORY	AMOUNT	BANKING WITHDRAWAL DENOMINATIONS					
		$1	$5	$10	$20	$50	$100
		DENOMINATION TOTAL					
(C) TOTAL	$						

SAVINGS/SINKING FUNDS

ACCOUNT	AMOUNT	Sinking Fund	Short Term	Long Term	Retirement
		☐	☐	☐	☐
		☐	☐	☐	☐
		☐	☐	☐	☐
		☐	☐	☐	☐
		☐	☐	☐	☐
		☐	☐	☐	☐
		☐	☐	☐	☐
		☐	☐	☐	☐
		☐	☐	☐	☐
		☐	☐	☐	☐
(D) TOTAL	$				

DEBT REPAYMENT

Record any payments in excess of the minimum payment due.

CREDITOR	PAYMENT	BALANCE
(E) TOTAL	$	

WEEK THREE SUMMARY

CATEGORY	AMOUNT
(A) Income Total	
(B) Bills & Expenses Total	-
(C) Cash Envelopes Total	-
(D) Savings/Sinking Funds Total	-
(E) Debt Repayment Total	-
NOTE: Subtract B/C/D/E from A to determine what's left. **What's Left**	=

WEEKLY SPENDING LOG

Use the Weekly Spending Log to determine what your current spending habits are. Review the log to assess and correct impulse spending.

DATE	TRANSACTION	AMOUNT	Planned/Budgeted	Impulse Purchase
			○	○
			○	○
			○	○
			○	○
			○	○
			○	○
			○	○
			○	○
			○	○
			○	○
			○	○
			○	○
			○	○
			○	○
			○	○
			○	○
			○	○
			○	○
			○	○
			○	○
			○	○
			○	○
			○	○
			○	○
			○	○
			○	○
			○	○
			○	○
			○	○
			○	○
			○	○
TOTAL		$		

Spending *Plan*

Week of:

INCOME		Salary/Wages	Investment	Business	Side-Hustle
INCOME SOURCE	AMOUNT				
Rollover from previous week		☐	☐	☐	☐
		☐	☐	☐	☐
		☐	☐	☐	☐
		☐	☐	☐	☐
		☐	☐	☐	☐
		☐	☐	☐	☐
		☐	☐	☐	☐
(A) TOTAL	$				

BILLS & EXPENSES		Cash	Credit Card	Debit	Check
PAY TO	AMOUNT				
		☐	☐	☐	☐
		☐	☐	☐	☐
		☐	☐	☐	☐
		☐	☐	☐	☐
		☐	☐	☐	☐
		☐	☐	☐	☐
		☐	☐	☐	☐
		☐	☐	☐	☐
		☐	☐	☐	☐
		☐	☐	☐	☐
		☐	☐	☐	☐
		☐	☐	☐	☐
		☐	☐	☐	☐
		☐	☐	☐	☐
		☐	☐	☐	☐
(B) TOTAL	$				

Financial Priorities

This week's financial goal(s)

CASH ENVELOPES							
CATEGORY	AMOUNT	BANKING WITHDRAWAL DENOMINATIONS					
		$1	$5	$10	$20	$50	$100
		DENOMINATION TOTAL					
(C) TOTAL	$						

SAVINGS/SINKING FUNDS

ACCOUNT	AMOUNT	Sinking Fund	Short Term	Long Term	Retirement
		☐	☐	☐	☐
		☐	☐	☐	☐
		☐	☐	☐	☐
		☐	☐	☐	☐
		☐	☐	☐	☐
		☐	☐	☐	☐
		☐	☐	☐	☐
		☐	☐	☐	☐
		☐	☐	☐	☐
		☐	☐	☐	☐
(D) TOTAL	$				

DEBT REPAYMENT

Record any payments in excess of the minimum payment due.

CREDITOR	PAYMENT	BALANCE
(E) TOTAL	$	

WEEK FOUR SUMMARY

CATEGORY	AMOUNT
(A) Income Total	
(B) Bills & Expenses Total	-
(C) Cash Envelopes Total	-
(D) Savings/Sinking Funds Total	-
(E) Debt Repayment Total	-
NOTE: Subtract B/C/D/E from A to determine what's left. **What's Left**	=

WEEKLY SPENDING LOG

Use the Weekly Spending Log to determine what your current spending habits are. Review the log to assess and correct impulse spending.

DATE	TRANSACTION	AMOUNT	Planned/Budgeted	Impulse Purchase
			○	○
			○	○
			○	○
			○	○
			○	○
			○	○
			○	○
			○	○
			○	○
			○	○
			○	○
			○	○
			○	○
			○	○
			○	○
			○	○
			○	○
			○	○
			○	○
			○	○
			○	○
			○	○
			○	○
			○	○
			○	○
			○	○
			○	○
			○	○
			○	○
			○	○
			○	○
TOTAL		$		

Spending *Plan*

Week of:

INCOME					
INCOME SOURCE	AMOUNT	Salary/Wages	Investment	Business	Side-Hustle
Rollover from previous week		☐	☐	☐	☐
		☐	☐	☐	☐
		☐	☐	☐	☐
		☐	☐	☐	☐
		☐	☐	☐	☐
		☐	☐	☐	☐
		☐	☐	☐	☐
(A) TOTAL	$				

BILLS & EXPENSES					
PAY TO	AMOUNT	Cash	Credit Card	Debit	Check
		☐	☐	☐	☐
		☐	☐	☐	☐
		☐	☐	☐	☐
		☐	☐	☐	☐
		☐	☐	☐	☐
		☐	☐	☐	☐
		☐	☐	☐	☐
		☐	☐	☐	☐
		☐	☐	☐	☐
		☐	☐	☐	☐
		☐	☐	☐	☐
		☐	☐	☐	☐
		☐	☐	☐	☐
		☐	☐	☐	☐
		☐	☐	☐	☐
(B) TOTAL	$				

Financial Priorities

This week's financial goal(s)

CASH ENVELOPES								
CATEGORY	AMOUNT	BANKING WITHDRAWAL DENOMINATIONS						
		$1	$5	$10	$20	$50	$100
		DENOMINATION TOTAL					
(C) TOTAL	$						

SAVINGS/SINKING FUNDS

ACCOUNT	AMOUNT	Sinking Fund	Short Term	Long Term	Retirement
		☐	☐	☐	☐
		☐	☐	☐	☐
		☐	☐	☐	☐
		☐	☐	☐	☐
		☐	☐	☐	☐
		☐	☐	☐	☐
		☐	☐	☐	☐
		☐	☐	☐	☐
		☐	☐	☐	☐
		☐	☐	☐	☐
(D) TOTAL	$				

DEBT REPAYMENT

Record any payments in excess of the minimum payment due.

CREDITOR	PAYMENT	BALANCE
(E) TOTAL	$	

WEEK FIVE SUMMARY

CATEGORY	AMOUNT
(A) Income Total	
(B) Bills & Expenses Total	-
(C) Cash Envelopes Total	-
(D) Savings/Sinking Funds Total	-
(E) Debt Repayment Total	-
NOTE: Subtract B/C/D/E from A to determine what's left. **What's Left**	=

WEEKLY SPENDING LOG

Use the Weekly Spending Log to determine what your current spending habits are. Review the log to assess and correct impulse spending.

DATE	TRANSACTION	AMOUNT	Planned/Budgeted	Impulse Purchase
			○	○
			○	○
			○	○
			○	○
			○	○
			○	○
			○	○
			○	○
			○	○
			○	○
			○	○
			○	○
			○	○
			○	○
			○	○
			○	○
			○	○
			○	○
			○	○
			○	○
			○	○
			○	○
			○	○
			○	○
			○	○
			○	○
			○	○
			○	○
			○	○
			○	○
	TOTAL	$		

Monthly Spending *summary*

Income	
Week One	
Week Two	
Week Three	
Week Four	
Week Five	
(A) TOTAL	$

Bills and Expenses	
Week One	
Week Two	
Week Three	
Week Four	
Week Five	
(B) TOTAL	$

Spending Assessment

Are there expenditures in your spending plan that can be cut or reduced? If yes, list the details below.

Cash Envelopes	
Week One	
Week Two	
Week Three	
Week Four	
Week Five	
(C) TOTAL	$

Savings/Sinking Funds	
Week One	
Week Two	
Week Three	
Week Four	
Week Five	
(D) TOTAL	$

Impulse Spending

Review the spending log for each week, then calculate the total amount of the transactions listed as impulse purchases.

$

Debt Repayment	
Week One	
Week Two	
Week Three	
Week Four	
Week Five	
(E) TOTAL	$

MONTHLY SUMMARY	
(A) Income Total	
(B) Bills & Expenses Total	-
(C) Cash Envelopes Total	-
(D) Savings/SF Total	-
(E) Debt Repayment Total	-
What's Left	=

Subtract B/C/D/E from A to determine what's left.

notes/observations

30-Day No Spend *challenge*

JAN FEB MAR APR MAY JUN JUL AUG SEP OCT NOV DEC

Place a check mark on the purse which corresponds to each day that you do not make an impulse or non-essential purchase.

Total number of no-spend days

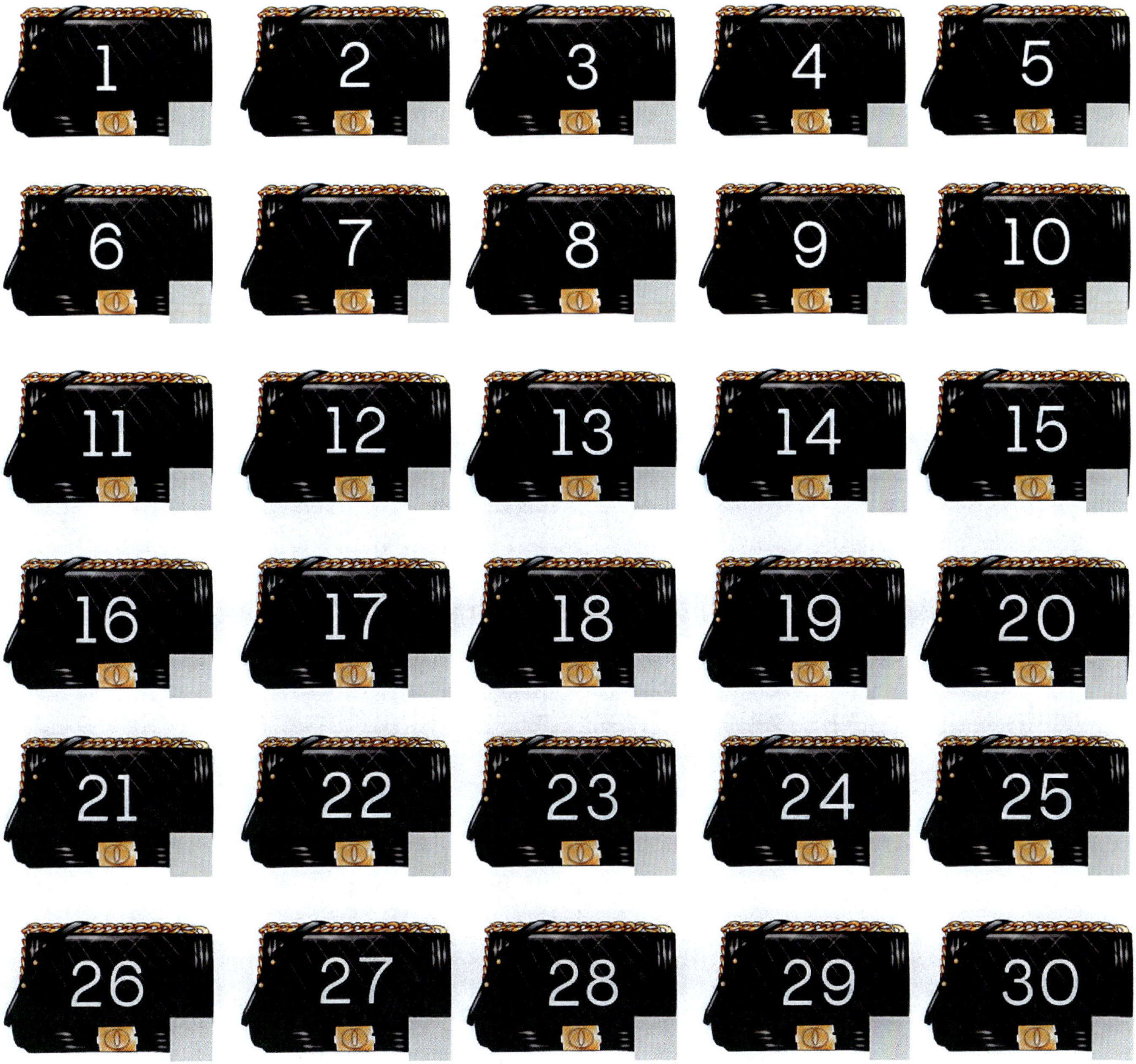

notes

Stay *focused*

"It's not how much money you make, but how much money you keep, how hard it works for you, and how many generations you keep it for."

Made in United States
North Haven, CT
04 November 2026

21725775R00119